£2 4 — 95.

The Heritage of Wisdom

THE HERITAGE
OF WISDOM

Essays in the History of Philosophy

Anthony Kenny

Basil Blackwell

Copyright © Anthony Kenny 1987

First published 1987

Basil Blackwell Ltd
108 Cowley Road, Oxford, OX4 1JF, UK

Basil Blackwell Inc.
432 Park Avenue South, Suite 1503
New York, NY 10016, USA

British Library Cataloguing in Publication Data
Kenny, Anthony
The heritage of wisdom: essays in the
history of philosophy
1. Philosophy—History
I. Title
109   B72
ISBN 0–631–15269–5

Library of Congress Cataloging in Publication Data
Kenny, Anthony John Patrick.
The heritage of wisdom
Includes index.
1. Philosophy—History. I. Title.
B29.K38 1987 190 87–11663
ISBN 0–631–15269–5

Typeset in 11 on 13 pt Baskerville
by Cambrian Typesetters, Frimley, Surrey
Printed in Great Britain by
T. J. Press Ltd., Padstow

Contents

Preface

This book is the fifth and last in a series of five volumes of my collected papers published over the years by Basil Blackwell, Oxford. The first, *The Anatomy of the Soul* (1973), contained a group of historical essays in the philosophy of mind, treating of Plato, Aristotle, Aquinas and Descartes. The second, *The Legacy of Wittgenstein* (1984), was a collection of essays partly about Wittgenstein's own work and partly about other philosophers whose strengths and weaknesses could be illustrated by a comparison with Wittgenstein's thought. The third, *The Ivory Tower* (1985), was subtitled 'Essays in Philosophy and Public Policy': the papers included in it dealt with the definition of murder in law, and the logic and ethics of nuclear warfare. The fourth, *Religion and Reason* (1987), was a collection of essays in philosophical theology, dealing with questions of method in religious thinking, with the existence and nature of God, and with the problems of grace, power and freedom.

This fifth volume contains a series of essays in the history of philosophy, ranging in subject matter from Aristotle to the present century, and written at various times during the last twenty years. As in the papers collected in *The Anatomy of the Soul* my aim has been not just to give an account of the work of some great thinkers of the past, but to draw upon their thought to cast light upon problems which remain on the philosophical agenda at the present time.

Thus, the first essay takes a problem much discussed recently – the role of luck in the moral life – and sets it against the background of comparable discussions in the writings of Aristotle and medieval Aristotelians. This paper was written as a contribution to a Festschrift for J. O. Urmson, forthcoming in 1987. The second paper, a brief overall account of Aquinas' writings and significance, first appeared in a Pan Books *A Dictionary of Philosophy* under the editorial supervision of A. N. Flew in 1979. The third and fourth papers concern central aspects of Aquinas' metaphysics and anthropology, respectively: the third was a contribution to a forthcoming Festschrift for Peter Geach, written in 1979; the fourth appeared in *Language, Meaning and God: Essays in honour of Herbert McCabe OP* (Chapman, 1987).

The fifth paper draws on the writings of the two greatest philosophers of the thirteenth century, Thomas Aquinas and Duns Scotus, to sketch the medieval origins of modern philosophy of mind. It was given as an invited lecture at the seventh international congress on medieval philosophy at Louvain-la-Neuve in 1982, and was published in 1986 in the proceedings of that conference, *L'Homme et son univers au moyen age*.

There follow two papers on the medieval philosopher and reformer John Wyclif. The first of the two was a Master Mind lecture to the British Academy, delivered in 1986, and published in the Academy's proceedings for that year. While this lecture gives a general view of Wyclif's thought and influence, the second piece is a more specialist essay on his philosophical realism as exhibited in his major treatise *De Universalibus*. It was first published in a collection of papers by various hands, *Wyclif in His Times*, which I edited for the Oxford University Press in 1986.

The eighth essay contrasts the theory of conscience held by the historical Sir Thomas More with the 'adamantine sense of self' of the hero of conscience in Robert Bolt's play *A Man for All Seasons*. It was given as a BBC talk with the title 'A Self out of Season' and was reprinted in the *Listener*, and in a Gollancz anthology *Good Talk* edited by Derwent May in 1968.

The first of the essays on Descartes also began life as a radio talk, for the BBC world service educational programme in 1978. Four other essays on Descartes deal with the two most popular topics of Cartesian scholarship: the Ontological Argument and the alleged circle in Descartes's refutation of scepticism. Essay ten was a contribution to a symposium at the first annual Philosophy Colloquium at the University of Western Ontario in 1966 and was published in the proceedings of that symposium edited by Joseph Margolis in 1969 under the title *Fact and Existence*. The eleventh essay is a response to comments and criticisms made on the tenth essay in the course of the symposium. I drew extensively on both papers in my book *Descartes: A Study of his Philosophy* (New York, Random House, 1968).

The paper 'The Cartesian Circle and the Eternal Truths' was a contribution to an American Philosophical Association symposium, with Alan Gewirth, in 1970; it was published in the *Journal of Philosophy* for 1970. The symposium gave rise to considerable further discussion in the journals. An Anglo-French philosophical colloquium gave me an opportunity to respond in the continuing debate in a paper 'The Cartesian Spiral' which was published in the *Revue Internationale de Philosophie* in 1983.

1

Aristotle on Moral Luck

Each of us must have had, at some time or other, the thought 'How lucky I am that I was not born in Nazi Germany.' The thought is not simply that one is lucky not to have been subjected to the sufferings of those who lived under Hitler: that one was not a prisoner in a concentration camp, for instance. It is also the thought that one is lucky not to have been subject to the temptation to take part in all the wickedness that was practised under the Nazis: that one was not, for instance, a guard in a concentration camp. 'I am lucky not to have been born in Nazi Germany,' we may think, 'because if I had been I might very well have turned out horribly wicked.'

The thought is a natural one, and yet it contains something of a paradox. How can a moral matter – such as whether someone turns out wicked or not – depend on luck? Philosophers often deny that it can: only what is within our control can be a proper subject for praise or blame; our moral responsibility cannot be affected one way or another by the good or bad luck involved in the consequences of our actions. Yet we are constantly meeting cases in practice where our evaluation of our own and others' actions does depend on their luck. A drunken driver, if he is lucky, may get home without doing any damage to himself or anyone else; if he is unlucky enough to encounter an incautious pedestrian, he may kill him. It will be a matter of luck, then, whether he faces charges of drunken driving or of homicide, if his journey has attracted the attention of the police. The law is likely to punish him quite differently in the two cases, and yet the risks he took were the same in each case. Is this an imperfection in the law? Should our moral evaluation be exactly the same in the two cases? Or is it morally worse to kill someone while driving drunk than to drive drunkenly home with fortunate impunity?

The topic of moral luck was introduced into philosophy in recent times by Bernard Williams and Thomas Nagel.[1] Williams takes his start from the classical ideal of happiness as the product of self-sufficiency: what is not in the domain of the self is not in its control and so is subject to luck and the contingent enemies of tranquillity. In such a tradition the good man was immune to what might be called incident luck; but it was a matter of what might be called constitutive luck that one was a sage or capable of becoming one. In more recent philosophical traditions the goal of making the whole of life immune to luck has been abandoned, but there remains influential the idea that one supreme value in life, moral value, can be thus regarded as immune: the successful moral life is a career open not merely to the talents but to a talent which all rational beings necessarily possess in the same degree. On this Kantian view, any conception of 'moral luck' is incoherent. Yet, Williams says, the aim of making morality immune to luck is bound to be disappointed. There is the constitutive luck which inescapably sets the conditions within which our moral dispositions, motives and intentions must operate. But there is also – and this is the focus of Williams's attention – the incident luck which is involved in bringing any project of moral importance to a successful conclusion.

Williams considers in detail the case of a creative artist, such as Gauguin, who turns away from pressing human claims to live a life in which he can best pursue his art. In such a situation the only thing that will justify his choice will be success itself; if he fails, he did the wrong thing. There is no way of giving, prior to the outcome of the project, a justification in terms of moral rules or of utilitarianism. So Gauguin's justification is a matter of luck: though not equally a matter of all kinds of luck. If he failed through an accidental injury, that would not necessarily mean that he was

---

[1] 'Moral Luck', *Proceedings of the Aristotelian Society, supplementary vol. 90 (1976), pp. 115–51*. A revised version of Williams's paper appears in his collection *Moral Luck* (Cambridge, Cambridge University Press, 1981) and of Nagel's in his *Mortal Questions* (Cambridge, Cambridge University Press, 1978). Subsequent references are to these revised versions.

wrong in his choice. What would prove him wrong in his project would not just be that it failed, but that he failed. Some luck is intrinsic to a project and some extrinsic; in Gauguin's case the intrinsic luck concentrates on whether he is a genuinely gifted painter who can succeed in doing genuinely valuable work. Intrinsic luck need not always lie within the agent, or the agent's control: the intrinsic luck involved in Anna Karenina's decision to leave her husband for Vronsky, for example, is something whose locus involves Vronsky as well as Anna.

Williams examines in detail cases such as these in which an agent's eventual evaluation of her own decisions and actions will be decided partly by the good or bad luck she has had in the execution of *her* projects. He concludes that luck cannot be eradicated from the moral sphere, however much of a scandal this may be for the Kantian conscience. 'Scepticism about the freedom of morality from luck cannot leave the concept of morality where it was.'[2]

Nagel is more reluctant to consider jettisoning the post-Kantian concept of morality; though he fully recognizes both that luck is ineliminable from the moral sphere, and that there is deeply rooted in our concept of morality the idea that one cannot be more culpable or estimable for anything than one is for that fraction of it which is under one's control. He sees the problem as parallel with scepticism about knowledge: if we take strictly the criteria which seem to distinguish cases where claims to knowledge are justified, we seem left knowing nothing; if we take seriously the criteria for restricting the application of responsibility, responsibility seems to shrink to a point. The search for value which is non-accidentally good seems as doomed as the search for belief which is non-accidentally true. 'The view that moral luck is paradoxical is . . . a perception of one of the ways in which the intuitively acceptable conditions of moral judgement threaten to undermine it all.'[3]

The view that good or bad luck should not influence moral assessments was strikingly put in a famous passage of Kant's:

If it should happen that by a particularly unfortunate fate or by the niggardly provision of a stepmotherly nature, the good

[2] *Moral Luck*, p. 39.
[3] *Mortal Questions*, p. 27.

will should be wholly lacking in power to accomplish its
purpose, and if even the greatest effort should not avail it to
achieve anything of its end, and if there remained only the
good will . . . it would sparkle like a jewel in its own right.[4]

Nagel observes, in comment on this passage: 'However jewel-like
the good will may be in its own right, there is a morally significant
difference between rescuing someone from a burning building and
dropping him from a twelfth storey window while trying to rescue
him.'[5]

Nagel identifies four ways in which the natural objects of moral
assessment are subject to luck:

> One is the phenomenon of constitutive luck – the kind of
> person you are, where this is not just a question of what you
> deliberately do, but of your inclinations, capacities and
> temperament. Another category is luck in one's circumstances
> – the kind of problems and situations one faces. The other two
> have to do with the causes and effects of action: luck in how
> one is determined by antecedent circumstances and luck in
> the way one's actions and projects turn out.[6]

I do not follow Nagel in thinking that free human actions can be
determined by antecedent circumstances, so I shall not consider
further his third kind of moral luck. The first, constitutive luck, is a
matter of the kind of person one is at the beginning of one's moral
life: this will depend partly on heredity and partly on environment
in proportions which nobody knows and everyone feels strongly
about. Fortunately we need not settle the proportion, since both
agencies have already done their worst before the individual is old
enough to become a moral agent. The second we may call
situational luck; the last kind listed by Nagel we may call executive
luck. So we have three kinds of moral luck: constitutive, situational,
executive. (Situational and executive luck are varieties of incident
luck.)

Neither Williams nor Nagel claims to be able to reconcile the

---

[4] *Groundwork of the Metaphysic of Morals*, p. 3 (Prussian edition, p. 394) tr. H. J. Paton.
[5] *Mortal Questions*, p. 25.
[6] *Mortal Questions*, p. 28.

phenomenon of moral luck with the tradition in moral philosophy since Kant. Williams seems to view this cheerfully: he is happy to tap a further nail into the coffin of Kantian morality. Nagel sees the problem as merged into a greater overall one about human agency: how are we to relate the view of a moral agent with the view of a self as a thing in the world and acts as events?

I do not claim to be able to reconcile what Williams and Nagel have shown to be so far asunder. Instead, I want to look at the problem of moral luck from within a different moral tradition, that of Aristotle. For though in modern times the topic of luck in morality was hardly discussed before the Williams–Nagel symposium, it was a topic that aroused interest in antiquity and, in a disguised form, in the middle ages. This paper, which is purely exploratory, is an attempt to relate what has been said in the modern debate to its ancient and medieval antecedents.

The form which the treatment of moral luck takes in the *Nichomachean Ethics* is a discussion of the relationship between luck and *eudaimonia*, which is roughly happiness. In chapter 10 of the first book Aristotle asks whether a man can be called 'happy' in his lifetime. Solon's dictum 'wait to see the end' does not mean that it is the dead who are really happy: that is absurd, particularly if happiness is defined, with Aristotle, as the activity of the soul in accordance with virtue. Perhaps it means that it is not safe to call a man happy until he is dead and beyond the reach of misfortune: but this too seems open to objection. 'Is it not paradoxical that at a time when a man actually is happy this attribute, though true, cannot be applied to him?' (*EN* 1100a34–35).

The reason that we are reluctant to call a man happy during his life is that misfortune may befall him. But it is quite wrong, Aristotle says, to make our judgement depend on fortune, 'for fortune does not determine whether we fare well or ill, but is, as we said, merely an accessory to human life; activities in conformity with virtue constitute happiness' (1100b8–10). It is true that no state which is not durable deserves to be called happiness; but activities in accordance with virtue are the most durable and invulnerable of human activities. Fortune can impede the activities of virtue and thus mar supreme happiness; but a happy man can never be made wretched by fortune.

The man who is truly good and wise will bear with dignity whatever fortune may bring, and will always act as nobly as circumstances permit, just as a good general makes the most strategic use of the troops at his disposal, and a good shoemaker makes the best shoe he can from the leather available, and so with experts in all other fields. If this is so, a happy man will never become miserable; but even so, supreme happiness will not be his if a fate such as Priam's befalls him (1100b35–1101a8).

If a man is equipped with all that is necessary for the exercise of perfect virtue at the present time, then he is happy. But he is supremely happy only if this state of affairs is going to continue until death, which we do not know. It will be true, then, that the word for supreme happiness, *makarios* or blessed, is something which cannot be safely applied until a life is complete. And even those who finally deserve the accolade will not be blessed as the gods are: their happiness, even if in the end it survives intact, being a merely human thing will have been forever vulnerable throughout life (1101a15–21).

This familiar passage of the *Nichomachean Ethics* is relevant to moral luck because happiness is a moral concept for Aristotle: or rather, the concept of a worthwhile life which is expressed by the word *eudaimonia* includes as an element what we should call moral excellence. But Aristotle does not here discuss directly the relationship between luck and moral virtue: the good man on the rack may, because of his misfortune, cease to be happy (1096a1–2), but there is no question of his ceasing to be virtuous (1100b22–33).

It is not surprising, perhaps, that we find no treatment of executive luck in the *Nicomachean Ethics*. We can at least guess what Aristotle would say about executive bad luck, the case where a moral agent, pursuing a worthwhile end, fails to achieve it because something goes wrong with the execution of his plan. If what goes wrong is something entirely external and incidental, then perhaps he is in the position of Priam, unable now to exercise the kingly virtues because of the collapse of Troy. But if what goes wrong is something intrinsic to his project – which was the case which Williams took as the paradigm of moral luck, and illustrated by the case of Gauguin's failing in his Tahitian project because he cannot bring off the kind of painting for which he has sacrificed everything else – this is something which Aristotle will not count as ill-luck at all. According to him, the exercise of virtue involves not only moral excellence but also wisdom; so a person of good intentions who fails to translate them into virtuous deeds will lack wisdom and thus not be really virtuous. A Gauguin who threw up everything to develop his artistic talent in the South Seas, and then turned out to have only an extremely mediocre talent to develop, would be, for Aristotle, not somebody suffering from moral ill-luck but somebody lacking the self-knowledge which is an essential part of wisdom. Aristotle's attitude here seems to me correct. Even if we are prepared, as Aristotle no doubt would not have been, to regard the pursuit of artistic excellence as a proper overriding aim for a man's life, it is essential that the pursuit should be based on a sound estimate of the artist's talent if it is to be deserving of any moral respect.

There is perhaps, however, not a great difference between Williams's approach here and the one I have attributed to Aristotle. For Williams agrees that if Gauguin turns out to be unable to produce paintings of value then he is morally unjustified in what he did. He might claim to differ from Aristotle only in taking a more realistic view of the degree of uncertainty in which human decisions have to be taken, a degree of uncertainty which no wisdom can altogether eliminate.

So much, then, for incident moral luck in the *Nicomachean Ethics*. Constitutive luck receives one brief mention in the final book (1179b20–23). 'Some people believe that it is nature that makes men good, others that it is habit, and others again that it is teaching. Now, whatever goodness comes from nature is obviously not in our power, but is present in truly fortunate men as the result of some divine cause.' True good luck is to receive, from a divine source, the gift of whatever may be the natural element in virtue.

It is in his lesser known ethical treatises that Aristotle treats the topic of moral luck at the length it deserves. In the middle ages one of the most popular Latin versions of Aristotle was a small treatise called the *De Bona Fortuna*, popular enough to survive in a hundred and fifty manuscripts (compared with fifty-five of the *Magna Moralia* in Latin, and not a single complete Latin one of the *Eudemian Ethics*). It is composed of extracts from the *MM* (2.8) and from the *EE* (VIII, 2). It has been published only partially;[7] the part of it which corresponds to the *Eudemian Ethics* provides a better source for the reconstruction of the Greek original than do the surviving Greek manuscripts of the *EE* which are in these passages corrupt.

According to the general Aristotelian theory, common to both the *Nicomachean* and *Eudemian Ethics*, happiness or welfare (*eudaimonia, eu prattein*) consists in the exercise of excellence which involves the operation of both wisdom in the intellectual part of the soul and moral virtue in the appetitive part of the soul. The discussion in the *De Bona Fortuna* (*EE* VIII, 2) starts from the consideration that not only wisdom produces happiness, but luck appears able to do so; and in general luck seems able to bring about the same results as knowledge. So we must inquire into the nature of good luck (*eutuchia*). Is it, for instance, by nature that one man is lucky and another unlucky? (1246b37–1247a3)

It seems beyond doubt that there are lucky people. There are those who do well in games of chance, and there are those who excel in matters like generalship and navigation, where skill is important, but where chance also has a major role. Now is being lucky an acquired disposition (*hexis*) like a virtue or a skill? Or is it something you are born with, like blue or brown eyes? (1247a3–12)

It is clear that luck is not a skill or species of wisdom; if it were, people would be able to give reasons for their lucky breaks. Is luck, then, a matter of divine favour: is being lucky a matter of having a guardian angel or *daimon* to pilot you through life? But why should God or an angel show special favour except to those who are best and wisest in their own right? (1247a12–30)

Well, if luck is not a matter of skill or of divine guidance shall we say that it is something naturally inborn? But nature acts with regularity, while good luck is unexpected and irregular. Luck is contrasted with nature, so that if nature made people strike lucky – as having eyes of a certain colour makes you see better or worse –

[7] Henry Jackson, 'Eudemian Ethics VIII 1, 2', *Journal of Philology* 32 (1912).

then they should be called not *eutucheis* but *euphueis*. A lucky man is one to whom chance brings good things; but if luck comes by nature is it not nature, rather than chance, that is the cause of these goods? (1247a29–62)

We meet a difficulty then in each of the hypotheses that we have explored: that luck is a skill, or a divine guidance, or a natural endowment. Shall we say then that there is no such thing as luck, and nothing is caused by luck? Is the notion of luck a cloak for our ignorance of causes? No: if there were an unknown cause in operation it would act with regularity; whereas luck is something which may strike once and not again. So, in spite of the difficulties, we must maintain that there is such a thing as luck and that it is a cause (1247b3–18).

The key to the problem is this. There are in the soul impulses of two kinds: there are those which are the outcome of reasoning, and there are others which are more primitive and prior to reasoning, originating in unreasoning appetite. Just as there is a natural impulse expressed in the desire for pleasure, so there is a natural appetite for every kind of good. Just as there are some naturally musical people who sing well without being taught music, so there are some who without reason are impelled in nature's way and desire what they ought, when they ought, and as they ought. These people succeed, though they lack wisdom and reason, just as people can sing well without lessons. There will be one kind of lucky people, then, who are those who succeed in general, without reasoning; and these will indeed be people who are naturally lucky (1247b18–28).

But this is not the only kind of good luck. When things turn out lucky, what is done is sometimes in accordance with desire and choice; sometimes it is not, but may be even contrary to it. In the first case it is because the reasoning was incorrect that we say the people were lucky; in the second case the luck consists in obtaining a good which in one way or another you did not desire. In the first case we can indeed speak of natural luck: it was the goodness of the natural desire which kept the person out of trouble; similar reasoning joined to evil desire might have led to misfortune. This case, then, is natural good luck; but in the other case there is no desire, so we cannot say that good luck here is due to natural rightness of desire. So there must be at least two kinds of luck (1247b28–1248a15).

The crucial question is: what is the cause of a person's having the desire for the right thing at the right time? If luck is the cause of this, then it looks as if luck is the cause of everything, including thought and deliberation. We cannot say that deliberation is the cause of deliberation, under pain of setting off on an infinite regress. So what is the starting point of what goes on in the soul? (1248a15–25) 'The answer is clear: as in the universe, so there, God moves everything by mind: for the divine element in us is in a manner the cause of all our motions. The starting point of reason is not reason but something superior to reason. What could be superior even to knowledge and mind, except God?' (1248a25–9)

There are some who, without reasoning, succeed in their projects; it does not pay them to deliberate because they have within them a principle that is better than mind and deliberation: inspiration (*enthousiasmos*). In swiftness and sureness of judgement such people are not outdone by the wise and learned; they make use of the divine to give them foresight of the future (1248a29–b3).

'It is clear', Aristotle concludes, 'that there are two kinds of good fortune: one divine, in which it appears the lucky man succeeds through divine aid – this is the person who succeeds in accordance with his impulse, while the other is he who succeeds against his impulse. Neither owes his success to reason. The former kind is more continuous good fortune, the latter is not continuous' (1248b3–7).

This chapter in Aristotle presents many difficulties. In the first place, the text is often corrupt, and emendations can only be conjectural even with the aid of the better text of the *De Bona Fortuna*. In the second place, the argument is often cryptic, and in particular it is difficult to see which of the many distinctions Aristotle makes are meant to be equivalent to each other, and which are intended to further subdivide classes already divided.

There appear to be four possible classes of people who are candidates for being *eutucheis*. First, there are those to whom God gives a good nature, which leads, via reasoning, to virtuous action. These are the normally virtuous people: though the original gift of good nature is something outside their power, it is the whole foundation of moral virtue. This is the constitutive good luck of which the *EN* speaks; it is mentioned at 1248a17–29 but it is not really regarded as a case of luck here. Then there is a case where God gives good nature, which leads via bad reasoning to successful outcome: here it is the initial good natural desire which is the case of the successful outcome (1247b37). Here too we are not really dealing with luck.

The third and fourth cases are the two cases which Aristotle regards as genuine cases of luck, and lists as the two kinds at the end of the chapter. The third is where God gives us inspiration which leads from good desire to good outcome, where there is no reasoning, but something which is more valuable than deliberation. It may be that Aristotle here has in mind the unreasoned decisions which Socrates attributed to his *daimon* and which preserved him from wrongdoing. It is this which is described as divine luck in the *EE*, not the constitutive luck so described in the *EN*. This is continuous good luck (which means that it is only doubtfully worthy of the name, since irregularity is taken by Aristotle as one of the characteristics of luck). Finally we have the case where somebody with bad desires performs good actions. This is a kind of luck; it is the non-divine, irregular kind mentioned last of all by Aristotle.

In the *EN* and *EE*, then, Aristotle recognizes constitutive and executive luck as contributing to virtuous behaviour. Situational luck is not mentioned in either as contributing to virtue: but it is mentioned in the *EN* as relevant to happiness – what Priam lacks is situational luck. But this kind of luck is in fact relevant also to virtue. It is a matter of luck whether we are placed in situations where we have to choose between being a hero and being wicked, instead of being able to steer a judicious course between the two as we usually do. (As in the case of someone forced by terrorists at gunpoint to plant a bomb; or a shipwrecked sailor who judges he can only survive by killing and eating the cabin boy.)

The constant reference to God in Aristotle's discussion of moral luck shows us where we should look for medieval treatments of the same topic. Aristotle's pagan luck is the equivalent of the Christian notion of divine grace. Divine luck, like divine grace, is a gift of God in humans, prior to all desert and the basis on which success or failure in the good life, salvation or damnation, is built. Grace is of several kinds, as Aristotle's luck is. There is the constitutive grace of being born and brought up in a Christian community; the sanctifying grace symbolized by baptism. The thoughts and primitive desires which precede all deliberation and choice and are the expression of the divine in us correspond to what theologians call actual graces. The inspirations which specially favoured people like Socrates receive correspond to the *gratiae gratis datae* with which some of the saints are favoured, such as Joan of Arc.

Christianity is often contrasted with Aristotelian morality as being more egalitarian. The elitist picture of the *megalopsychos* in the *EN*, who needs wealth and power to display the greatness of his soul, is contrasted with the gospel religion of the poor and humble, equal citizens of the Kingdom of God.

The basic unfairness of the world is altered by Christianity, but it is not in fact eliminated. The widow's mite, we are told, is as valuable in the sight of God as the gift of the rich man: so the unequal opportunities for practising munificence are evened out *sub specie aeternitatis*. But the unfairness of the distribution of terrestrial wealth has as its counterpart the inequality of access to heavenly riches. According to traditional Christian teaching, it makes a great difference to one's chances of salvation whether one is born before or after the arrival of the Messiah, into a Godfearing Christian family or into a pagan milieu as part of a *massa damnata*.

The feature of moral luck which is most offensive to our modern notions is its opposition to the ideals of equality. Constitutive luck contrasts with the ideal of equality of talent, which very many people would like to be true, and which some people actually believe to be true. Situational luck contrasts with the ideal of equality of opportunity, which seeks to place people as far as possible in equal situations. (Equality of opportunity was originally pursued against a belief in inequality of talent; equality of opportunity was indeed designed to see that inequality of rewards matched inequality of skills, etc., and not inequalities of birth: the career was to be open to the unevenly distributed talents.) Executive luck points up the inequality of human achievement, both absolutely and in relation to desert.

The conflict between luck and inequality seems more painful

given that the history of morality shows an ever greater weight being placed on the ideal of equality. The topics covered in Aristotle's *Ethics* include much more than we would naturally think of as moral: there are the virtues of courage, wisdom, temperance, as well as the virtue of justice. In the middle ages the virtues of faith, hope and charity, none of which have anything to do with equality, occupied the centre of the moral stage. We have gradually equated morality with the area covered by the cardinal virtue of justice; and even within the range of justice we have concentrated on distributive justice to the exclusion of retributive and other forms of justice, placing need rather than desert in the centre of the picture.

When the notion of morality is thus circumscribed, and when morality is regarded as the supreme human value, the tension between luck and morality becomes excruciating. If, from an Aristotelian viewpoint, the Kantian type of moral value is seen only as one among others, then the tension is relaxed a little: the inequality of distribution of the wherewithal for moral goodness is perhaps no more and no less a scandal than the inequality of distribution of the wherewithal for intellectual achievement or artistic creation. But the inequality of the distribution of all these gifts is something that never ceases to disquiet us.

The parable of the talents does not suggest that there is a basic equality of the most valuable human gifts; its moral is rather to reject discouragement in the development of a comparatively modest talent. The parable of the labourers in the vineyard suggests that however much effort one puts into the cultivation of these gifts, the distribution of achievement will in no way reflect the distribution of desert.

Neither ancient paganism nor medieval Christianity nor modern secularism has done anything to defer the conclusion that the world operates on principles quite other than those of fairness, and that no human institutions can radically alter the basic unfairness of the world.

Still, though we cannot eliminate it, we do try, at our best moments, to make our social arrangements compensate for the unfairness of the world in the distribution of non-moral goods. We try to raise the most disadvantaged to – not equality, but – a minimum tolerable level of distribution of the goods accessible to society. We give special education to the intellectually subnormal, we give social assistance to the economically deprived, we make special provisions for access and mobility for the physically handicapped. Can we, and should we, make similar attempts to diminish the moral unfairness of the world?

Let it be observed first of all that there is nothing *unjust* in the operation of moral luck as I have described it. Moral luck, I have said, offends against our intuitions about responsibility and our sense of fairness. But the offence against responsibility would only be a genuine one if the recognition of moral luck involved holding people responsible for things where they had no choice about the outcome. It would be the moral equivalent of strict liability. But one can recognize moral luck without doing that. In law there is not simply the stark alternative between strict liability and restricting punishment to deliberate wrongdoing. The law punishes negligent and reckless wrongdoing as well as intentional crime: and what is thus punished is a mixture of choice and luck. Even when we punish the unfortunate Nazi guard or IRA accessory, we are not punishing people who had no choice in the matter of their misdeeds. They had a difficult choice and the correct choice would have been a heroic choice; but none the less they had a choice, and they did what they did knowing that they were doing wrong and what the outcome would and could be.

The two principal ways in which the recognition of moral luck seems unfair are these.

We sometimes hold people equally responsible for equal deeds done under circumstances of unequal temptation: as we find guilty of murder the IRA accessory as well as the cold-blooded murderer who was under no similar pressure. This is a case of situational bad luck.

We sometimes hold unequally responsible people who performed equally culpable acts (or were guilty of equal reprehensible negligences) when they have unequally bad outcomes (we don't find the lucky drunken driver guilty of manslaughter). This is a case of executive bad luck.

Is there injustice here? Let us consider first the question of deserts. There is injustice when someone gets less than their deserts, or is punished more than they deserve. That is not in question in either case: the driver is punished for the risk he took, and gets no more than he deserved; the lucky driver gets better than he deserves, but there is no injustice in this and it is supported by the principle of economy of punishment. So with the coerced accessory: he is guilty of murder, having preferred his own skin to someone else's, and there is good deterrent reason against letting him go.

But in addition to the justice which assigns just measure in accordance with deserts, is there not distributive justice, which aims at an equal or at least equitable distribution of goods? And should we not, in the interests of fairness, try to achieve a fair distribution of moral good as we do of the goods of health and strength and wealth?

Once one reflects on it, one sees that the goal of making everyone morally equal has not the *prima facie* attractiveness of making everyone equally rich, clever and powerful. In fact, distributive justice has no application to the distribution of moral goodness. But with moral goodness as with other forms of goodness we do indeed wish to diminish the effect of luck. We should aim to take the maximum benefit to society from the good luck of those who are morally lucky, and minimize the damage to society of those who are morally unlucky. To make our morality blind to the effects of luck would have exactly the opposite effect: if we marked down the lucky, we would diminish their incentive for using their luck on our behalf; if we let off the unlucky altogether we would deprive them of their incentive to heroism.

A rational morality then is closer to the Aristotelian than to the Kantian one. Of morality as a whole we can say what Aristotle said of the good man: that he is like the cobbler who makes the best shoe with the bad leather he has. The best morality then is one that makes the best of the unfair world we live in. It is not one which denies the unfairness of the actual world, nor one which pursues fairness and equality in an imaginary metaphysical world of pure morality and pure good will.

2

The Achievement of Thomas Aquinas

Thomas Aquinas was born about 1225 at Roccasecca near Aquino in Italy. He was schooled by the Benedictine monks of Monte Cassino and studied liberal arts at the University of Naples. Against the bitter hostility of his family he joined the Dominican Order of begging friars in 1244 and studied philosophy and theology at Paris and at Cologne under Albert the Great. From 1254 to 1259 he lectured at Paris, becoming a full professor ('regent master') in 1256. During the decade 1259–69 Aquinas was in Italy, occupying various posts in his order and in the service of the Popes at Orvieto, Rome and Viterbo. From 1269 to 1272 he taught for a second period at Paris during a period of lively theological and philosophical controversies in the University. His teaching career ended due to ill health in 1273 after a year at the University of Naples where he had begun his career as an undergraduate. He died at Fossanova on March 7 1274 while journeying to Lyons to take part in the Church Council there. Three years after his death a number of propositions representing his views were condemned by ecclesiastical authorities in Paris and Oxford; but in 1323 he was canonized by Pope John XXII at Avignon and in 1879 Pope Leo XIII issued an encyclical commending his works to Catholic scholars.

Aquinas' works, though all written within twenty years, are enormously voluminous. Best known are his two massive syntheses of philosophy and theology, the *Summa contra Gentiles* (*Against the Errors of the Infidels*) which by itself is sixty thousand words longer than the whole corpus of Berkeley's philosophy, and the *Summa Theologiae* which expounds his mature thought at even greater length. These encyclopaedic works, though theological in intent and, largely, in subject matter, contain much material that is philosophical in method and content. The earliest of Aquinas' theological syntheses, his commentary on the *Sentences* of Peter Lombard, then a century old, is the least philosophically rewarding to read. Most explicitly philosophical is the series of commentaries on Aristotle (on the *Analytics*, *De Anima*, *De Caelo*, *Ethics*, *De Interpretatione*, *Metaphysics* and *Physics* and parts of the *Politics*) and a number of pamphlets written during his Paris sojourns for teaching or polemical purposes (such as the *De Ente et Essentia*, a juvenile work on being and essence, the *De Principiis Naturae* on the causes of change in nature, the *De Unitate Intellectus* attacking the Averroist view that the whole of mankind has only a single intellect, and the *De Aeternitate Mundi* arguing that philosophy cannot prove that the cosmos had a beginning in time). Among the most lively of Aquinas' remains are the *Quaestiones Disputatae*, records of live academic debates on a variety of theological and philosophical topics such as truth (the *De Veritate*), divine power (the *De Potentia*), the soul (the *De Anima*) and free choice (the *De Malo*). Matter of philosophical interest can be found even in Aquinas' commentaries on books of the Bible, such as his exposition of the Book of Job.

Aquinas wrote a dense, lucid and passionless Latin which though condemned as barbaric by Renaissance taste can serve as a model of philosophical discourse. The majority of his works are now available in English translation.

Aquinas' first service to philosophy was to make the works of Aristotle known and acceptable to the Christian west, against the lifelong opposition of conservative theologians who were suspicious of a pagan philosopher filtered through Muslim commentaries. Aquinas' commentaries on the translations of his friend William of Moerbeke made students in western universities familiar with Aristotle's own ideas, and in his theological writings he showed to what a considerable extent it was possible to combine Aristotelian positions in philosophy with Christian doctrines in theology. Though his principal philosophical themes and techniques are Aristotelian, Aquinas was no more a mere echo of Aristotle than

Aristotle was of Plato. In addition to working out the relationship between Aristotelianism and Christianity Aquinas develops and modifies Aristotle's ideas within the area of philosophy itself. Thus, for instance, the part of the *Summa Theologiae* devoted to general ethical questions (the *Prima Secundae*) expounds and improves upon Aristotle's account of happiness, virtue, human action and emotion before going on to relate these teachings to the specifically theological topics of divine law and divine grace.

Naturally Aquinas' philosophy of physics has been antiquated by the progress of natural science, and his philosophy of logic has been rendered archaic by the development of mathematical logic and the reflection of philosophers and mathematicians in the hundred years since Frege. But his contributions to metaphysics, philosophy of religion, philosophical psychology and moral philosophy entitle him to an enduring place in the first rank of philosophers.

In metaphysics Aquinas applied the Aristotelian distinction between actuality and potentiality to a wide variety of topics and problems. If we consider any substance, such as a piece of wood, we find a number of things which are true of that substance at a given time, and a number of other things which, though not true of it at that time, can become true of it at some other time. Thus, the wood, though it *is* cold, *can be* heated and turned into ash. Aristotelians called the things which a substance *is* its actualities, and the thing which it *can be* its potentialities: thus the wood is actually cold but potentially hot, actually wood, but potentially ash. The change from being cold to being hot is an accidental change which the substance can undergo while remaining the substance that it is; the change from wood to ash is a substantial change, a change from being one kind of substance to another. The activities involved in changes are called 'forms': accidental forms if involved in accidental change; substantial forms if involved in substantial change. 'Matter' is used as a technical term for what has the capacity for substantial change.

All terrestrial objects, Aquinas believed, consisted of matter and form. But in addition to these composite entities there were pure forms: angelic beings with no particle of matter in their composition. The principle of individuation for terrestrial beings – what makes two things of a kind two and not one – is matter: two peas in a pod may resemble each other as much as you like, but they are two peas and not one because they are two different parcels of matter. Angels, having no matter, can never be two of a kind: one angel differs from another as a man differs from a dog; each angel is a species of its own.

Aquinas sometimes speaks, particularly in his juvenile works, as if the coming of something into existence was another case of the actualization of a potentiality like a pint of milk turning into butter: a non-existent essence acquires the actuality of existence. In his more mature thinking on the topic, he insisted that the creation of beings could not be regarded as the actualization of shadowy essences in this way. But he continued to use the terminology of essence and existence to mark a distinction between God and creatures: in all creatures essence and existence were distinct (for the creatures might never have existed) while in God essence and existence were one (for God's existence is necessary in a unique sense). Aquinas' writing on *esse* or existence is a strange mixture of insight and confusion: the confusion has not prevented his theory of Being from becoming an object of great admiration among his followers.

The doctrine of matter and form spills over from Aquinas' metaphysics into his philosophy of mind in a number of ways. Forms can exist in two ways: with *esse naturale* (i.e. as the form which makes a piece of matter the kind of thing it is) or with *esse intelligibile* (i.e as an idea in someone's mind). Moreover, the human soul is the form of the human body: it is the possession of human life and human powers which make a particular parcel of matter the body it is. Against theological opposition Aquinas insisted that the rational soul is the *only* substantial form of the human body: for this he was condemned after his death by those who believed in a hierarchy of souls, intellectual, animal and vegetable, plus a form of corporeity. This archaic dispute has its contemporary counterpart in the debate whether memory or bodily continuity is the criterion of personal identity.

The two principal powers of the human soul, for Aquinas, are the intellect and the will. The intellect is the capacity to think: to form concepts and to possess beliefs. Concepts and beliefs are called by

Aquinas '*species*', an ambiguous term with the many senses of the English word 'idea'. The intellect is the power to acquire, possess and exercise *species*: the power to acquire them, by operating upon sense-experience, is called the active intellect (*intellectus agens*) and the power to store and exercise them is called the receptive intellect (*intellectus possibilis*). Against Muslim commentators on Aristotle, Aquinas maintained that every individual human being possessed both kinds of intellect; and against Platonizing theologians he insisted that for both the acquisition and the exercise of intellectual ideas the cooperation of the imagination was necessary. The imagination he considered as a type of interior sense-faculty, providing objects for the intellect to contemplate and modify.

Aquinas' theory of the will builds on the theory of voluntariness, choice and human action familiar to readers of Aristotle's *Nicomachean Ethics*. Aquinas improves on Aristotle by developing a concept of intention (intermediate between Aristotle's concepts of voluntariness and choice) and by having a work-out theory of conscience. His detailed and subtle analysis of the elements of human free choice and action is one of the most easily comprehensible and permanently valuable features of his philosophy.

Aquinas' most famous contribution to the philosophy of religion is his Five Ways or proofs of the existence of God. Motion in the world, Aquinas argues, is only explicable if there is a first unmoved mover; the series of efficient causes in the world must lead to an uncaused cause; contingent and corruptible beings must depend on an independent and incorruptible necessary being; the varying degrees of reality and goodness in the world must be approximations to a subsistent maximum of reality and goodness; the ordinary teleology of non-conscious agents in the universe entails the existence of an intelligent universal Orderer. Several of the Five Ways seem to depend on antiquated physics, and none of them has yet been restated in a way clear of fallacy. The more valuable part of Aquinas' natural theology is his examination of the traditional attributes of God, such as eternity, omnipotence, omniscience, benevolence, and his exposition and resolution of many of the philosophical problems which they raise. In the wider area of philosophy of religion Aquinas' most influential contribution was his account of the relationship between faith and reason and the independence of philosophy from theology. Faith is a conviction as unshakeable as knowledge, but unlike knowledge not based on rational vision; the conclusions of faith cannot contradict those of philosophy but they are neither derived from philosophical reasoning nor are they the necessary basis of philosophical argument. Faith is, however, a reasonable and virtuous state of mind because reason can show the propriety of accepting divine revelation.

Even after his canonization Aquinas did not enjoy in the middle ages that official status in the Catholic Church which has been accorded to him in modern times. Most medieval Thomists were Dominicans, and it was only in the period between the First and the Second Vatican Council that the study of Thomist doctrines was enjoined as a regular part of the education of all Catholic clergy. The official sanction given to Aquinas' work by Catholic authorities was an obstacle to the serious critical study of his philosophy: many Catholics tended to study textbooks 'according to the mind of the Angelic Doctor' rather than reading his own writings; non-Catholics shied away from him as being the spokesman for a party line. Text-book Thomism presented theories such as the analogy of Being, the doctrine of natural law, the real distinction between essence and existence, which represented hardenings of a fluid and nuanced position in Aquinas himself. But in recent decades the work of dedicated medievalists, secular as well as Christian, and the waning of official Catholic Thomism has begun to make room for a just appreciation of Aquinas' genius based upon purely philosophical criteria.

3

Form, Existence and Essence in Aquinas

In the present century few philosophers in philosophy departments in British universities have made any very serious study of medieval philosophy: scholastic writers such as Aquinas have been read rather by historians and theologians. Those few who have taken a strictly philosophical interest in medieval thinkers owe a great debt to Peter Geach for his writings on Aquinas and on later medieval logicians, and most recently for his work as General Editor of the edition of Paul of Venice being prepared under the auspices of the British Academy.

My own debt to Geach in the area of medieval philosophy is particularly great. Before meeting him in Oxford I had been trained in Rome in scholastic philosophy as presented in seminary textbooks, but I had read little medieval philosophy at first hand. Indeed I regarded scholastic systems as dull and dead by comparison with the living excitement of analytic philosophy. It was above all from Geach that I learnt the importance of distinguishing between Aquinas and his twentieth-century admirers: I grew familiar with the pocket edition of the *Summa* which he kept always to hand, and came to envy his phenomenal memory for passages of the text. I learnt too that some of the most apparently crabbed and arcane topics of medieval disputation were, beneath the surface, very closely linked to items of contemporary debate. One of the most stimulating essays in the history of philosophy I have ever read was Geach's 1955 Aristotelian Society lecture, 'Form and Existence'.

The lecture contains a useful comparison between Frege's theory of functions and Aquinas' theory of forms. Just as Frege regarded a predicate, such as '. . . is a horse', as standing for a particular kind of function, namely a concept, so Aquinas held that a general term such as 'horse' standing in predicate position referred to a form. The form which is referred to by the predicate in the sentence 'Socrates is wise' may be referred to also by the phrase 'the wisdom of Socrates'; but this latter expression must not be construed as 'wisdom, which belongs to Socrates', just as 'the square root of 4' does not mean 'the square root, which belongs to 4'. 'The wisdom of Socrates', in Geach's terminology, refers to an *individualized* form; the expression which indicates the generic form, the form strictly so called, is not 'wisdom' nor 'the wisdom of Socrates' but 'the wisdom of . . .' (cf. *S. Theol.* Ia 3, 2 ad 4; Ia 50, 2). 'Wisdom' *tout court* means nothing in heaven or earth; wisdom is always *wisdom of*; as Aquinas put it, it is of something (*entis*) rather than itself something (*ens*). Against Plato's doctrine that the form signified by a general term is 'one over against many', Aquinas insisted that the question 'one or many' is itself only intelligible if we ask it in relation to a general term that signified a form or nature.

Geach admits that the account which he gives of individualized forms does not accord in all respects with Aquinas' language; but it is a most interesting analysis in its own right, whether or not it is to be found in its worked out form in Aquinas' writings. Geach treats Aquinas as Aquinas treated Aristotle – improving his insights, tactfully masking his confusions, charitably resolving his ambiguities. This may exasperate historians, but it is the philosophically rewarding way to read a classic text. But in some cases Geach benignly interprets Aquinas in a way which fathers on Aquinas ideas and arguments which are not his and of which he might well have disowned the paternity.

One such case is the distinction which Geach maintains between an individualized form and the *esse* of that individualized form. This distinction he attributes to Aquinas and defends by reference to Aquinas' writings. The distinction, it seems to me, is not to be found in Aquinas in the terms in which it is propounded by Geach.

It is, however, related to a distinction which is undoubtedly to be found in Aquinas: the distinction, in every creature, between essence and existence. The distinction between individualized form and *esse* is related to this distinction, but it is not the same distinction, since the essence of a human being, such as Socrates, is something really distinct both from Socrates and from his substantial form or soul. It includes matter, flesh, bone, as well as the soul of Socrates, though it does not include any particular bit of matter, flesh or bone. But Geach's arguments for the distinction between individualized forms and their *esse* would, if valid, provide reasons for a parallel distinction between individualized essences and the existence corresponding to each of them.

The distinction between individualized forms and *esse* was first set out and argued for in 'Form and Existence' in 1955; arguments were set out at greater length, and some objections to them were countered, in Geach's contribution on Aquinas in the Anscombe–Geach volume *Three Philosophers* (Blackwell, 1961). In what follows, I quote 'Form and Existence' from the text reprinted in my anthology *Aquinas: A Collection of Critical Essays* (Macmillan, 1969).

In order to show that any individualized form is really distinct from the corresponding *esse* Geach presents three arguments drawn from Aquinas' writings. The first may be called the argument from the shareability of natures; the second, the argument from intensive magnitude; and the third, the argument from intentional existence. None of the arguments, in my view, succeeds in establishing Geach's distinction between *esse* and form or Aquinas' distinction between essence and existence.

The first argument is thus stated by Aquinas in a well-known passage of the *Summa Theologiae* (Ia 3, 5: *Tertio* . . .) to show that God is in no genus.

All members of a genus share the quiddity or essence of the genus which is predicated of them in the category of substance. But they differ in respect of *esse*, for a horse's *esse* is not the same as a man's, and this man's *esse* is not the same as that man's. So wherever something belongs to a genus its quiddity or essence differs from its *esse*. In God, however, as has been shown, there is no such difference. Clearly, therefore, God is not a species within a genus.[1]

Aquinas' language here does not suggest that he is talking about an *individualized* form or essence. If horse and rider can be said to share animality, and Peter and Paul to share humanity, then on the face of it the animality and humanity in question are not individualized but general. If Aquinas was talking about individualized humanities, he could say not just that this man's *esse* differs from that man's but also, with equal right, that this man's humanity is distinct from that man's. What is being distinguished from *esse* in this passage appears to be not the individualized form, Peter's humanity, but rather Humanity as such.

Geach paraphrases Aquinas' argument in such a way as to avoid this Platonic implication.

> If *x* is F and *y* is F, then in respect of F-ness *x* and *y* are so far alike; the F-ness of *x* will indeed be a different individualized form from the F-ness of *y*, but they will be, as F-nesses, alike. But when *x is* and *y* also *is*, the *esse* of *x* and the *esse* of *y* are in general different as such. (p. 49)

Geach illustrates the sense in which the *esse*s of two individual substances are in general distinct by contrasting the normal situation with an imaginary one in which several substances share a single *esse*.

> In the fairy-tale, all the human members of the family and the family cat shared a single life, that is, a single *esse* (*vivere viventibus est esse*); and when the betrothed of the youngest daughter took a pot-shot at the cat, its death was the death of the whole family. In actual families, animality is common to all the members of the family, including the cat, but *esse* is not, and so killing the cat has no such consequence. (p. 50)

[1] Tertio quia omnia quae sunt in genere uno communicant in quidditate vel essentia generis quod praedicatur de eis in eo quod quid. Differunt autem secundum esse, non enim idem est esse hominis et equi, nec huius hominis et illius hominis. Et sic oportet quod quaecumque sunt in genere differant in eis esse et quod quid est, idest essentia. In Deo autem non differunt, ut ostensum est. Unde manifestum est quod Deus non est in genere sicut species.

It is difficult to see why Geach describes the lot of the fairy-tale family by saying that they all share a single *esse* or life, rather than by saying that their several lives and *esses* were bound together by a common destiny such that they would all end together. When father, mother and daughter simultaneously die, the Registrar General even of fairyland will surely add three deaths, not one, to his statistics. We can, if we like, say that they all shared a common death, like the passengers in an aeroplane crash: but they share a common death only in the same sense in which they share a common humanity. If we want a rule for individuating and counting deaths, surely the most natural rule is to say that there are as many deaths as there are individuals that die. In just the same way, if we insist on counting humanities, it seems that we must say that there are as many humanities as there are individuals that are human.

It is hard to know whether Aquinas would give the same reason as Geach for saying that this man's *esse* is not the same as that man's. Passages parallel to Ia 13, 5 (e.g. *De Ente* 6; *De Potentia* 7, 3) do not elaborate. In the *Summa contra Gentiles* we read: 'Whatever belongs to a genus differs in respect of *esse* from other things in the same genus; otherwise a genus would not be predicable of many things' (I, 25). In the fairy-tale family there are many animals: in so far as *esse* is a predicate, it is predicable of each of them; it is the *esse* of *many animals*. There is no distinction between *esse* and generic predicates to be found along these lines.

In *Three Philosophers* Geach presents a more developed form of the same argument.

In view of Aquinas' doctrine of universals, it is hard to see the force of his saying that two men or two animals 'share in a quiddity or essence'. So far as his words go, he might well have been taken to argue that since the *esses* are different while the quiddity is the same, the quiddity of each man or animal must differ from the *esse* – only this cannot be his mind, since for him the humanity of this man is not identical with the humanity of that man, and the animality of a man is even unlike that of a horse. We should rather, I think, construe his argument thus: 'while the quiddities (the animalities) of two animals are certainly different, this difference arises from the side not of quiddity but of *esse*; were there not difference of *esse*, there could be but one individualized animality in two animals even of different species; as there is but one individualized animality in the two kidneys of a given animal, or again in his kidney and liver, differently organized as these are.' (p. 94)

Several things are puzzling about this intriguing suggestion: it is a pity that Geach did not develop it at greater length. To say that if two animals did not have a different *esse* they could not have a different undividualized animality, just as two kidneys of a given animal have only one individualized animality, is to suggest that the two kidneys have a single *esse*. But one kidney may die or be removed while the other kidney continues to function; yet hitherto Geach has taken the possibility of X's ceasing to exist while Y continues to exist as establishing that X and Y have different *esse*s. Moreover, in what sense is there an individualized animality *in* a kidney? In the passage just quoted from Aquinas it is clear that he has in mind a principle according to which F-ness is in a thing if and only if 'F' is predicable of the thing. But 'animal' is not predicable of a kidney: a kidney is not an animal. If there is such a thing as kidneity, there are presumably two kidneities, and not just one, in a pair of kidneys.

To be sure, the functioning of an animal's kidneys is part of its functioning as an animal; and on Aquinas' view the whole animal functioning of the human being Peter is organized by a single form, Peter's substantial form or intellectual soul (Ia 76, 3). In this, quite different, sense one might speak of animality as being 'in' a kidney (for on Aquinas' view the animality of Peter is one and the same form as the humanity of Peter, though of course animality differs from humanity). It might seem therefore that we could establish a distinction between form and *esse* by appealing to the case of kidney transplantation. If Peter's kidney is transplanted into the body of Paul, do we not have a case of a single kidney, with a single *esse*, informed first by the animality of Peter and then by the animality of Paul? I am inclined to think that Aquinas would regard the transplanted kidney as being only by a figure of speech the same kidney before and after the transplant: as being a piece of matter informed first by Peter's soul (which organizes the matter into one kidney) and then by Paul's soul (which organizes the matter into another, different kidney). But whether or not this is the correct way to explain to topic on Thomist principles, the transplantation does not provide an instance of a difference between an individualized form and the *esse of that same form*. If there is such a thing as a form of kidneity, that lasts just as long as the kidney lasts; while if we are talking about the individualized humanities of Peter and Paul, then it is the *esse* of Peter and Paul's souls, not the *esse* of any shared kidneys, that is relevant to the problem of the real distinction. Neither in its original nor in its modified form does Geach's first argument give us any grounds for distinguishing between an individualized form and that by which the individualized form *is* or continues in existence.

A more promising argument is drawn from the consideration of intensive magnitude.

> It may be that x is F and y is F, and that they have the same specific F-ness, but yet the F-ness of x is more intense than that of y. Moreover, the F-ness of x may become more or less intense; and increase of F-ness plainly resembles a thing's coming to be F, whereas a decrease of F-ness resembles a thing's altogether ceasing to be F. Now difference between x and y as regards intensity of F-ness is not difference precisely as regards F-ness (especially as we may suppose x and y to have the same specific F-ness); it is rather, I wish to say, difference as regards the existence of F-ness – the F-ness of x exists more than the F-ness of y. So also a change in mere intensity is a change as regards existence; increase in the intensity of x's F-ness resembles the coming to be of x's F-ness, both being additions of existance; decrease in the intensity of x's F-ness resembles the ceasing of x's F-ness, both being subtractions of existence. Here again, there is a real distinction between the F-ness of x and the *esse* of this individualized form; while the F-ness as such remains unchanged, its existence may vary in degree.

Geach gives no reference to Aquinas for this argument; but there are to be found in the *Summa Theologiae* two lengthy treatments of intensive magnitude, one in connection with forms and dispositions in general (Ia IIae 52), one in connection with the particular case of the theological virtue of charity (IIa IIae 24). The theory presented in those two passages seems to disagree in some important respects with the argument presented by Geach.

Aquinas says of charity that its *esse*, like that of any accident, is to inhere in a substance. (*'Accidentis esse est inesse'* is a common slogan in his writings: where 'F' is an accidental predicate, the existence of a particular F-ness is simply something's being F.) Hence, he goes on to say: 'for charity to increase in respect of its essence is one and the same thing as its inhering to a greater degree in its possessor. It increases essentially not by beginning or ceasing to be in its possessor, but because it begins to be to a greater degree in its possessor' (IIa IIae 24, 5 ad 3). He is not saying that the charity as such remains unchanged while the *esse* varies in degree, as Geach would have him say; he is saying rather that the change in the essence of the charity is the very same thing as a change in the degree of its existence in its possessor. And so with all forms which admit of variation in intensity: 'This is the mode of increase proper to every form which is intensified, because the *esse* of such a form consists in its entirety in its inhering in its possessor (IIa IIae 24, 5c).

Whether or not Geach's argument corresponds to Aquinas' mode of speaking in passages such as these, it is an interesting one which deserves consideration in its own right. One difficulty which arises is this: if the temperature of water in a kettle rises from 98° Centigrade to 99° Centigrade, how are we to decide whether this consists in the departure of one form (the form of *being 98° hot*) and its replacement by another (the form of *being 99° hot*) or whether it is simply an increase of *esse* in one and the same form, hotness? Geach recognizes that there are difficulties in treating an increase of heat as an instance of the intensification of a form; but he goes on to say: 'So far as I can see, *sound* is a good example. A louder and a softer sound may be qualitatively identical; and a sudden increase of loudness resembles a sound's suddenly starting, a sudden decrease of loudness its suddenly stopping' (1969, 51).

But in a similar manner we can ask, when the sound of A flat on the flute increases during a crescendo from n descibels to n + 2 decibels, whether here we have a case of the intensification of a single form or the replacement of one form by another. The reply would no doubt be that wherever we have the possibility of *continuous* increase or decrease in the intensity of a quality it is more intelligible to regard the change as a variation in *esse* than as the rapid succession of an infinite series of infinitesimally differing forms. In *Three Philosophers* Geach remarks in this context that Hume was wrong to draw the conclusion that all the degrees of a given quality are perfectly distinct from one another like different colours or tones.

In this case, then, there seems to be good reason to distinguish between an individual form and the *esse* of that individual form. But as Geach admits, the argument lacks generality: a shape, or a relation like fatherhood, or a substantial form, does not admit of differences in intensity. This point is made, with respect to various forms and essences, by Aquinas himself in a number of places. For instance:

> The criterion for assigning something to a species must be hard and fast and precise. There are therefore two things which may make it impossible for a form to be possessed in differing degrees. First, the form may be what qualifies its possessor for membership of a species. No substantial form can be possessed in different degrees. That is why Aristotle says that just as number does not admit of more or less, neither does substance in the sense of species (i.e. there is no *more* nor *less* in the possession of specific form) . . . Secondly, it may be that precision is part of the notion of a particular form, so that if anything possesses that form, it must possess it altogether or not at all. That is why specific numerical terms cannot have 'more' or 'less' added to them: each specific term or number is made up of indivisible units. The same is true of specific terms assigning numerical measurements to continuous quantities ('two cubits long', 'three cubits long') and of relational terms ('double' 'treble', etc.) and of terms assigning shape ('triangular', 'quadrilateral', etc.) (Ia IIae 52, 1c).

Thus Geach's second argument, if valid, establishes a distinction between an individualized form and its *esse* only in the case of those forms that admit of being possessed in varying degrees. In other cases it cannot establish the distinction: in particular, it cannot be used to establish any distinction between the individualized essence of a substance and that substance's *esse*.

The third argument offered by Geach, however, is one of unrestricted generality. It is based on the distinction between a form as thought of, and a form as existing in nature; and since whatever can exist can be thought of, if the argument works in one case it will work in all cases.

The argument is based on Aquinas' theory of intentionality, which is stated by Geach in the following manner:

What makes a sensation or thought of an X to be *of an X* is that it is an individual occurrence of that very form of nature which occurs in an X – it is thus that our mind 'reaches right up to the reality'; what makes it to be a *sensation* or *thought* of an X rather than an actual X or an actual X-ness is that X-ness here occurs in the special way called *esse intentionale*, and not in the 'ordinary' way called *esse naturale*.

So for Geach we have not just similarity but identity of forms. To be sure, my thought of a horse and the form of that horse grazing in the field are two *occurrences* of the form; but they are two occurrences of the *same* form, every bit as much as two occurrences of the form of horse in two horses grazing side by side. So we must distinguish between the form and its *esse*.

To evaluate this argument we must remember that while form is the object of knowledge, actual individuals, for Aquinas, are composed of form and matter. And because it is matter which is the principle of individuation, the form which is grasped by the intellect is universal, unlike the individual accidental forms which are the objects of sense-perception.

This feature is neglected in Geach's presentation of the theory that the form of the thought is the same as the form of the object of thought. Geach argues that we must make a real distinction between form and existence: in the case of each individualized form there is a distinction between the form and its *esse*. But Aquinas' doctrine of intentionality does not provide grounds for such a distinction, contrary to what Geach says. It is no part of Aquinas' doctrine that there is one same individualized form of horse which occurs in a particular horse, say Eclipse, with *esse naturale*, and occurs also in my mind with *esse intentionale*. What we have are two different individualizations of the same form, not two different existences of the same individualized form. The form, in the mind, is individuated by its thinker.

Geach writes: 'When Plato thinks of redness, what exists in Plato is not a certain *relation* to redness or red things, but *is* redness, is an individual occurrence of the very same form of which another individual occurrence is the redness of this rose.' There is an equivocation in the sense of 'individual occurrence' here. The occurrence of redness in a particular rose is an individual occurrence because it is an occurrence of redness in a particular rose: it is the redness of *this rose*. The occurrence of redness when Plato thinks of redness is not individual by being the thought of the redness of any particular thing, but by being a thought by a particular thinker, namely Plato. It was a constant doctrine of Aquinas that thought, as such, is not directly of individual things at all, neither of individual forms like the redness of Socrates nor of individual substances like Socrates himself (e.g. *S. Th.* Ia 86, 1).

Hence, Geach's arguments fail to establish a distinction between individual form and *esse*. Most importantly, Geach's arguments lend no support to the celebrated Thomistic doctrine of the real distinction between essence and existence.

In my view, Aquinas' teaching on essence and existence rests on a confusion between generic and individual essences. Aquinas thought that in all creatures essence and existence were distinct, whereas in God the two are identical. If we understand 'essence' in the generic sense (corresponding to a Fregean function such as '. . . is God', '. . . is a human being'), then the doctrine of the real distinction between essence and existence is the truism that whether or not a concept is instantiated is quite another matter from what are its constituent characteristics; but the doctrine that the two are identical in God is the nonsense that the question 'What kind of thing is God?' is to be answered by saying 'There is one.' On the other hand, if we understand 'essence' in the individual sense in which we can speak of the individualized humanity possessed by Socrates and by Socrates alone, then the doctrine of the real distinction in creatures becomes obscure and groundless. As Aquinas often insists, for a human being to exist is for it to go on being a human being; Peter's existing is the very same thing as Peter's continuing to possess his essence; if he ceases to exist he ceases to be a human being, and his individualized essence passes out of the nature of things.

To expose in detail the confusion in the doctrine of essence and existence would take us beyond the limits of a short paper. I have tried to do so elsewhere. The confusion which I have tried to expose is one of which I would never have become aware had I not been taught, by Geach's *Form and Existence*, to keep a sharp eye open for the distinction between generic and individualized forms.

4

Aquinas on Knowledge of Self

Aquinas has a problem in giving an account of how a human intellect knows itself. Intellectual knowledge, for him, is immaterial; but matter is the principle of individuation. Hence, he concludes, intellectual knowledge is primarily only of universals; individuals can be known only secondarily and indirectly by the intellect. How, then, can a human intellect be immediately aware of itself, since any such intellect is itself a particular individual? The present paper attempts to outline how Aquinas tried to solve this problem, and to assess how far he succeeded in doing so.

In Aquinas' account of these matters, a crucial role is played by the relationship between the intellect and the imagination. According to article 7 of question 84 of the first part of the *Summa Theologiae*, the two faculties are intimately interrelated. The issue raised in the article is whether the intellect can exercise intellectual activity using only the intelligible species in its possession without turning to phantasms.[1] The answer given is that in the present life the intellect cannot exercise intellectual activity upon anything at all unless it turns itself towards the phantasms.

Let us begin by decoding the arcane terminology. Aquinas' '*intellectus*' is fairly enough translated by the English word 'intellect': it is the capacity for understanding and thought, for the kind of thinking which differentiates humans from animals; the

---

[1] Utrum intellectus possit actu intelligere per species intelligibiles quas penes se habet non convertendo se ad phantasmata.

kind of thinking which finds expression especially in language, that is, in the meaningful use of words and the assignment of truth-values to sentences. But English does not have a handy verb, 'to intellege', to cover the various activites of the intellect, as the Latin has the verb '*intelligere*' for what the intellect does. To correspond to the Latin verb one has to use circumlocutions, as above I used 'exercise intellectual activity' to correspond to '*actu intelligere*'. An alternative would be to use the English word 'understanding' in what is now a rather old-fashioned sense, to correspond to the name of the faculty, '*intellectus*', and to use verb 'understand' to correspond to the verb '*intelligere*'. In favour of this is the fact that the English word 'understand' can be used very widely to report, at one extreme, profound grasp of scientific theory ('only seven people have ever really understood special relativity') and, at the other, possession of fragments of gossip ('I understand there is to be a cabinet reshuffle before autumn'). But 'understand' is, on balance, an unsatisfactory translation for '*intelligere*' because it always suggests something dispositional rather than episodic, an ability rather than the exercise of an ability; whereas '*intelligere*' covers both latent understanding and current conscious thought. When Aquinas has occasion to distinguish the two he often uses '*actu intelligere*' for the second: in such cases the expression is often better translated 'think' than 'understand'.

What, next, are 'intelligible species'? These are the acquired mental dispositions which are expressed, manifested, in intellectual activity: the concepts which are employed in the use of words, the beliefs which are expressed by the use of sentences. My grasp of the meaning of the English word 'rain' is one kind of species; my belief that red night skies precede fine days is another kind of species. The most natural English word to cover both concepts and beliefs is 'idea', and in some contexts 'idea' makes an unproblematic equivalent for '*species*'. But in the present context it might be misleading, since the British empiricist philosophers used the word 'idea' for mental images, which are something quite different from *species intelligibiles*.

Mental images are called by Aquinas 'phantasms' (*phantasmata*). A visual image, called up when one's eyes are shut; the words one utters to oneself *sotto voce* in the imagination: these are clearly examples of what he means by 'phantasm'. How much else is covered by the word is difficult to determine. Sometimes straight-forward cases of seeing events in the world with eyes open seem to be described as a sequence of '*phantasmata*': it is not clear whether this means that the word is being used broadly to cover any kind of sense-experience, or whether Aquinas held a regrettable theory that external sense experience was accompanied by a parallel series of phenomena in the imagination. For our purposes it is not necessary to decide between these alternatives: when Aquinas talks of '*phantasmata*' we can take him to be speaking of occurrences taking place either in the senses or in the imagination. For what he is anxious to elucidate is the role of the intellect within the sensory context provided by the experience of the sentient subject.

According to Aquinas, *phantasmata* are necessary both for the acquisition and for the employment of species. At birth the intellect is pure capacity, void of concepts and beliefs; these are acquired by abstraction from phantasms (Ia 85, 1). (Again, the analogy with the British empiricists suggests itself; again the analogy is misleading.) When a concept has been acquired, or when a belief has been formed, the intellect has taken a step from potentiality towards actuality; it is no longer a *tabula rasa*, but has a content; it is in possession of species. But this, according to Aquinas, is not sufficient to enable the intellect to operate unaided: phantasms are needed not only for gaining possession of species but also for making use of them.

Why so? Aquinas puts to himself the following objection:

> It would seem that the intellect can exercise intellectual activity without turning to phantasms, simply by using the species in its possession. For the intellect is placed in a state of actuality by a species informing it. But for the intellect to be in a state of actuality is precisely for it to exercise intellectual activity. Therefore species suffice to enable the intellect to exercise intellectual activity without turning to phantasms (Ia 84, 7, obj. 1).

The answer is to be found by distinguishing two stages of actuality. Possessing a concept or a belief is different from being totally uninformed; but it is different again from exercising the concept or calling the belief to mind. I may know French without, on a given date, speaking, reading or thinking French; I may believe that the earth is round even when my thoughts are on totally different things. The distinction, in terms of actuality and potentiality, may be made in more than one way. Knowing French is an actuality by comparison with the state of the newborn infant; it is a potentiality by comparison with the activity of actually speaking French. Sometimes Aquinas, and often later scholastics, distinguish the three stages as pure potentiality, first actuality, and second actuality. In these terms, the thesis of Ia 84, 7 is that phantasms are needed to take the intellect not only from potentiality to first actuality, but also from first actuality to second. Without the jargon, the thesis is that intellectual thought is impossible apart from a sensory context.

It seems to be possible to bring out the truth of this thesis even if one takes a starting point very different from that of Aquinas. According to one strand of modern philosophy, thought is essentially operating with symbols; and symbols are signs that bear meaning. Whatever account we are to give of the way in which meaning can be attached to signs, we cannot dispense with the signs to which the meaning is to be attached. The signs may be uttered sounds or marks on paper: entities perceptible by the senses. Or they may be items in the imagination, such as the words of a fragmentary interior monologue. Either way the signs will provide the sensory context for the intellectual thought.

Any thought must have two essential features: it must be a thought with a content, and it must be a thought with a thinker: it must be somebody's thought, and it must be a thought of something. What makes a thought a thought of something is its meaning, its intentionality; what makes a thought somebody's thought is its being an item in that individual's mental history rather than someone else's.

One may think by talking, whether aloud to others or in silence to oneself. What gives the thought its content, in such a case, is the meaning of the words used; and it is because we grasp that meaning that thinking is an activity of the intellect, which is, precisely, the ability to confer and understand meaning. When I think thus, what makes the thought *my* thought is, in the standard spoken case, that it is I who am doing the speaking; in the case of my talking to myself, it is the fact that those images are part of *my* mental history. It is thus that the occurrence of something perceptible by the senses, or something occurring in the imagination, is necessary if I am to have a thought; it is thus that intellectual activity involves *conversio ad phantasmata*.

Aquinas' own arguments for his thesis are rather different. He says that since the intellect is a faculty which uses no bodily organ, its operation could not be impeded by bodily injury unless some other faculty were involved. But human beings cannot use their minds if they are in a state such as a seizure or a coma. This must be because the intellect cannot act without the aid of the senses and the imagination which do have bodily organs (Ia 84, 7c).

Several things seem wrong with this argument. First, we want to know why Aquinas says that the intellect has no bodily organ. Why do not the phenomena he cites tell as much in favour of the thesis that the intellect has a bodily organ as in favour of the thesis that the intellect has need of the imagination? Aquinas might argue that the intellect does not have an organ in the way that the faculty of sight has, because there is no part of the body that one brings to bear in order to understand better, in the way that one moves and focuses one's eyes to see better. If so, it can be replied that in precisely the same sense of 'organ' there is no organ of imagination either: there is no part of our body which we bring to bear in order to imagine better. But 'organ' may be used in a broader sense, to mean any part of the body which is intimately related with the exercise of a faculty; so that, in this sense, the visual cortex would be an organ of sight no less than the eye. If so, why should we deny that there is an organ of the intellect? Is not the brain just such an organ?

Moreover, Aquinas' argument makes it appear as if the need for thought to take place in a sensory context is a contingent matter. This is something which is not uncongenial to him, since he wishes to defend the possibility of thought in disembodied souls. But if the considerations outlined above are correct, the connection between thought and imagination seems to be a necessary rather than a contingent matter.

Aquinas' second argument for his thesis also seems flawed. It goes thus:

> Everyone can experience in himself, that when someone tries to understand (*intelligere*) something, he forms for himself some phantasms by way of examples in which he can, as it were, look at what he is trying to understand. That is also why when we want to make someone else understand something, we offer him examples from which he can form phantasms for himself in order to understand . . . If it is to exercise its proper activity about its proper object, the intellect must turn to phantasms, to intuit the universal nature existing in the particular (Ia 84, 7c).

The line of argument here suggests that the relation of species to phantasm is the same as that of universal to particular. But this is not so, for several reasons. I can have a concept of horse which is not the concept of any particular horse; but equally I can have an image of a horse which is not an image of any particular horse. When I use instances and examples to help grasp a difficult proposition, the instances and examples may be general no less than particular. Thus, suppose I am wondering about the correctness of the logical principle:

If every x has the relation R to some y, then there is some y to which every x has the relation R.

In such a case I will no doubt call up instances and seek for counterexamples. But the propositions I would call to mind – for example 'every boy loves some girl', 'every road leads to some place' – though less general than the logical principle I am using them to test are none the less universal and not particular.

But though Aquinas' arguments seem doubtful, his conclusion seems, as I have already argued, to be correct. Moreover, in answering the third objection to his thesis, he makes a qualification to it which removes the most obvious argument that might be brought against it. The third objection runs thus:

There are no phantasms of incorporeal things, because the imagination does not go outside the world of time and the continuum. So if our intellect could not operate upon anything without turning to phantasms, it would follow that it could not operate upon anything incorporeal.

This conclusion would be, of course, quite unacceptable to Aquinas since he believed that we could have some understanding of God and immaterial angels. In his reply he explains that this understanding, though genuine, is limited. Incorporeal substances are known negatively and by analogy.

Incorporeal things, of which there are no phantasms, are known to us by comparison with empirical bodies of which there are phantasms . . . to understand anything of things of this kind we have to turn to phantasms of empirical bodies, even though there are no phantasms of them.

Aquinas is perhaps too pessimistic about the possibility of there being images of non-bodily things. After all, surely Michelangelo's Sistine *Creation does* contain an image of God. What is true is that the image of a non-bodily thing is not an image of it in virtue of resembling it. But there is good reason to believe that what makes an image of X an image of X is *never* its resemblance to X, even if X is bodily. Be that as it may, Aquinas' answer to his objection does make the valid point that even if it is true that one cannot think of anything without an image, it does not follow that one cannot think of X without an image *of X*. When we think by talking to ourselves, if we talk to ourselves about X, the most common image which will be the vehicle of our thought about X will not be an image of X (visual, say), but an image (most likely auditory) of the word for 'X'. But of course it may be an image of many other things too, and there are many ways of thinking about X which do not involve talking to ourselves.

According to the thesis defended in article 7 of question 84, imagery, or a sensory context, is necessary for thought of any kind, including the most abstract, metaphysical, or theological thought. But when we turn to consider thought about concrete individuals –

the kind of thought expressed by a proposition such as 'Socrates is mortal' – then the senses and the imagination are involved in an even more intimate way. This is spelt out in two stages. In article 3 of question 85 Aquinas asks whether our intellect knows what is more universal before it knows what is less universal; in article 1 of question 86 he asks whether our intellect knows individuals.

There is, as we have said, a special problem for Aquinas about intellectual knowledge of individuals because of his thesis that individuation is by matter. Some philosophers have thought that an object could be individuated by listing the totality of its properties. Since to have a property is to fall under some universal – to be square, for instance, is to be an instance of the universal 'square' – if an item can be individuated by its properties, all we need to identify an individual is to list the universals under which it falls. But Aquinas rightly rejected this: in theory, however long a list of universals we draw up, it is always logically possible that more than one individual will answer to the list.

One of Aquinas' clearest statements on this topic occurs in the second question of *De Veritate*, in article 5, where the topic is God's knowledge of singulars. According to Avicenna, Aquinas says, God knows each singular in a universal manner, by knowing all the universal causes which produce singulars.

> Thus, if an astronomer knew all the motions of the heavens and the distances between all the heavenly bodies, he would know every eclipse which is to occur within the next hundred years; but he would not know any of them as a particular individual, in such a way as to know whether or not it was now occurring, in the way that a peasant knows that while he is seeing it. And it is in this manner that they maintain that God knows singulars; not as if he intuited the singular nature of them, but by positing the universal causes.

But this account, Aquinas maintains, is quite inadequate, for the following reason:

> From universal causes nothing follows except universal forms, unless there is something to individuate the forms. But

however many universal forms you pile up, you never make them add up to anything singular. For it always remains possible to think of the totality of forms as being instantiated more than once.[2]

All this is well and clearly said, and it underlines Aquinas' problem. If the intellect – human, no less than divine – is a faculty for grasping universals, how can there be intellectual knowledge of a singular individual? The theses which set the problem are boldly stated in the discussion, in Ia 85, 3, of whether intellectual knowledge of the more universal is prior to intellectual knowledge of the less universal. The first thing to be said on this topic, according to Aquinas, is this:

> Intellectual knowledge in a certain manner takes its origin from sense knowledge. And since the object of the sense is the singular, and the object of the intellect is the universal, it must be the case that the knowledge of singulars, in our case, is prior to the knowledge of universals.[3]

We know the singular before the universal (for instance, when we are babies innocent of language); but our *intellect* can be said baldly to have as its object the universal alone. This seems correct. A child sees dogs long before it acquires the concept 'dog'; seeing is of the individual, because one cannot see a dog that is not any particular dog; the concept is of the universal, because there is no theoretical limit on the number of things which may fall under the description 'dog'.

But both in the case of the senses and of the intellect, Aquinas

[2] Si quis astrologus cognosceret omnes motus caeli et distantias caelestium corporum, cognosceret unamquamque eclipsim quae futura est usque ad centum annos; non tamen cognosceret eam in quantum est singulare quoddam, ut sciret eam nunc esse vel non esse, sicut rusticus cognoscit dum eam videt. Et hoc modo ponunt Deum singularia cognoscere; non quasi singularem naturam eorum inspiciat, sed per positionem causarum universalium . . . Ex causis universalibus non consequuntur nisi formae universales, si non sit aliquid per quod formae individuentur. Ex formis autem universalibus congregatis, quotcumque fuerint, non constituitur aliquid singulare; quia adhuc collectio illarum formarum potest intelligi in pluribus esse.

[3] Cognitio intellectiva aliquo modo a sensitiva primordium sumit. Et quia sensus est singularium, intellectus autem universalium; necesse est quod cognitio singularium, quoad nos, prior sit quam universalium cognitio.

says, more general precedes less general knowledge. From a distance you can tell that something is a tree before you can tell that it is a beech; you can spot a dog without being able to decide whether it is a labrador or an alsatian: you can see a man coming before you can recognize him as Peter or Paul. Here Aquinas appeals to the authority of Aristotle: 'Thus, at the beginning, a child distinguishes man from non-man before distinguishing one man from another; that is why, as Aristotle says, a child begins by calling all men "father" and only later distinguishes between each of them.' The illustration is not really very helpful, because one wants to know how Aristotle decides whether the child (a) means 'man' by 'father' or (b) means 'father' and believes that everyone he sees is his father.

The fact seems to be that in the case of a faculty such as a sense, which is a faculty for discrimination, the precise discrimination is, logically, subsequent to the imprecise discrimination; progress in discrimination is progress from the less determinate to the more determinate. But in the case of the intellect it seems we cannot make the same generalization. Sometimes we proceed from the more general to the less general, and sometimes in the opposite direction. We may acquire the concept 'tree' before learning the different kinds of tree; on the other hand, a child may have mastered 'dog' and 'cat' before he has the more general term 'animal', and in adult life it may take a degree of sophistication to regard both heat and light as species of a common genus.

But genus and species are related as more general and less general within the realm of the universal; according to the doctrine enunciated in the *De Veritate*, the relation between species and individual is quite different from that between genus and species. There is one surprising passage in article 4 of question 85 where it almost seems as if Aquinas has forgotten this. He says:

> If we consider the nature of genus and species as it is in individuals, we find that it stands in the relation of formal principle with respect to individuals; for the individual is individual because of its matter, it belongs to a species by virtue of its form. But the nature of the genus is related to the nature of the species in the manner of a material principle;

because the nature of the genus is taken from what is material
in a thing, the specific element from what is formal; as
animality is derived from the sensory part, and humanity from
the intellectual part.[4]

At first sight, this looks as if Aquinas is suggesting that genus is
related to species as species is related to individual. This would be
quite wrong, on his own principles: the two relationships cannot be
treated as parallel instances of the relation of indeterminate to
determinate. Genus is related to species as indeterminate to
determinate, indeed, but species is not related to individual as
indeterminate to determinate; as Aquinas spelt out in the *De
Veritate* passage above, no collection of determinations will individuate a particular.

But Aquinas is not saying that the individual is related to the
species as determinate to indeterminate. He is saying that in a
given individual the matter can be regarded, like genus, as
something indeterminate. Just as there is no animal that is not a
particular kind of animal – no animal which belongs to the genus
but to no species of the genus – so too there is no matter which is
not matter of a particular kind, matter informed by a specific form.
But it would be wrong to say that matter is to form as
indeterminate to determinate; the truth is that matter is to
informed matter as indeterminate to determinate.

It is in the brief first article of question 86 that Aquinas finally
gives his answer to the question whether our intellect knows
individuals. 'Directly and primarily', he says, 'our intellect cannot
know individuals among material things.'

The reason is that the principle of individuation in material
things is individual matter, and our intellect, as said before,
operates by abstracting intelligible species from that kind of
matter. But what is abstracted from individual matter is

[4] Si autem consideremus ipam naturam generis et speciei prout est in singularibus, sic
quodammodo habet rationem principii formalis respectu singularium: nam singulare est
propter materiam, ratio vero speciei sumitur ex forma. Sed natura generis comparatur ad
naturam speciei magis per modum materialis principii: quia natura generis sumitur ab eo
quod est materiale in re, ratio vero speciei ab eo quod est formale; sicut ratio animalis a
sensitivo ratio vero hominis ab intellectivo.

universal. Therefore our intellect has direct knowledge only of universals.

There was a time when I found this thesis shocking and incredible. Shocking, because if it is impossible to have intellectual knowledge of an individual, it must be equally impossible to have spiritual love for an individual; for the will can only relate to what the intellect can grasp. Hence love between human individuals must be mere sensuality. Incredible, because one of the time-honoured paradigms of intellectual activity is the formulation of syllogisms such as, 'All men are mortal; Socrates is a man; therefore Socrates is mortal.' But one cannot formulate singular propositions, in a real case, if one cannot understand what is meant by the individual terms which occur in them. How much preferable to Aquinas' teaching, I used to think, is the belief in the Scotist tradition that each individual has a *haecceitas*, a unique essence, which can be grasped as such by the intellect!

Later, however, I have come to see that Aquinas was right to maintain that our knowledge of material individuals cannot be something which is purely intellectual. This can be made clear if we reflect that the intellect is, above all, the human capacity to master language and to think those thoughts which are only expressible in language. There is no way in which we can uniquely identify an individual in language without going outside language itself and latching on to the context within which the language is used.

When I think of a particular human being, there will be, if I know her well, many descriptions I can give in language to identify who I mean. But unless I bring in reference to particular times and places there may be no description I can give which would not in theory be satisfiable by a human being other than the one I mean. As Aquinas emphasized in the *De Veritate* passage, I cannot individuate simply by describing a list of attributes. Only perhaps by pointing, or taking you to see her, can I settle beyond doubt which person I mean; and pointing and vision go beyond pure intellectual thought.

Similarly, if I bring in spatio-temporal individuating references I have left the realm of intellectual thought; from the point of view of a pure spirit there would be no such framework. It is only by

linking universal intellectual ideas with sensory experience that we
know individuals and are capable of forming singular propositions.
And that is what Aquinas says.

> Indirectly, and by a certain kind of reflection, the intellect can
> know an individual; because, as said above, even after it has
> abstracted species it cannot make use of them in intellectual
> operation unless it turns towards the phantasms in which it
> grasps the intelligible species, as Aristotle says. Thus, what
> the intellect grasps directly by the intelligible species is the
> universal; but indirectly it grasps individuals which have
> phantasms. And that is how it forms the proposition 'Socrates
> is a man'.

We come, then, finally to the question how, within this theoretical
framework, to account for knowledge of the individual self. The
question of self-knowledge can be put in more than one way. We
may ask: how does a human individual know himself? Or we may
ask: how does the human intellect know itself? Aquinas prefers, in
question 87, the second formulation. This is perhaps surprising in
view of his correct insistence elsewhere that it is a human being
who thinks and understands, just as it is a human being (and not,
say, an eye) which sees. Equally surprisingly, the first question
which he puts to himself, in connection with the intellect's self-
knowledge, is whether the intellect knows itself by its essence. We
may well wonder whether talk of the essence of an individual
intellect does not, in the end, involve Aquinas in believing in
something very like a Scotist *haecceitas*.

Let us postpone, for the moment, the question of the essence of
the individual intellect, and consider what St Thomas thought
about the essence of an individual human being. One might first try
to distinguish a Thomist individual essence from a Scotist *haecceitas*
by saying that it includes matter. But according to St Thomas the
essence of a human being does not include any individual matter
(*materia signata*); no particular parcel of matter, only some matter or
other. The essence of a human being is what makes him a human
being, which includes having a body; but the essence does not
include having *this* body, or a body composed of *this* matter. For St

Thomas as for Scotus there are individual essences; but whereas for Scotists it is the *haecceitas* which individuates, for the Thomist it is the other way round: the essence is individuated by its possessor. My soul, my essence, my intellect are the soul, essence, intellect they are, are the individual items they are, because they are the soul of Anthony Kenny, who is *this* body. Even if, as Aquinas thought, they can survive my death, they are still the individuals they are because they belonged to this *body*.

If we bear this in mind, we realize that my soul does not have an essence except in the sense that it is the spiritual aspect of *my* essence. If Aquinas asks whether the intellect knows itself by its own essence, it is not because he believes that it has an independent essence, but because that was what was believed by those Platonists whose view he is attacking here. If the human intellect were a pure spirit in contact with some world of pure Ideas, then its self-knowledge too would no doubt be some spiritual self-translucence. But *our* minds are not like that, at least in the present life.

> Our intellect becomes the object of its own intellectual activity in so far as it is actualized by species abstracted from empirical things by the light of the active intellect . . . So it is not by any essence of itself, but through its activity that our intellect knows itself (Ia 87, 1).

But intellectual self-knowledge is of two very different kinds. There is the individual's self-knowledge: Socrates perceives that he has an intellectual soul by perceiving his own intellectual activity. But there is also the human race's knowledge of what human understanding is: this is something gathered painfully by philosophic toil, and many human beings never rightly acquire it. The first kind of knowledge, Aquinas says, presents no such problem: 'In order to have the first kind of knowledge of the mind, the mind's own presence is sufficient, since it is the principle of the act by which the mind perceives itself.'

We may wonder, however, whether, on Aquinas' own principles, matters ought to be as simple as this. The intellect is a faculty for the grasping of universals: what is this 'perceiving' that we are now told is one of its activities? If it is a perceiving involving knowledge of an individual – namely the mind itself – it seems that it must operate indirectly, through reflection on phantasms. But we are given no account of how reflection on phantasms helps the mind to knowledge of that individual which is itself. Aquinas has explained that what makes a thought the thought of an individual object is its relation to phantasms which are related to that object. But what makes the thought the thought of an individual subject: i.e. what makes my thoughts *my* thoughts? It is not as if this – at first sight bizarre – question was not one which occurred to Aquinas. As I wrote a few years ago in an OUP *Past Master* on Aquinas:

> The question was a very lively one in Aquinas's time and the subject of much controversy between Latin and Arab inter-preters of Aristotle. Aquinas insisted, against the Averroists, that such a thought is my thought, and not the thought of any world-soul or supra-individual agent intellect. But to the question what makes them *my* thoughts his only answer is the connection between the intellectual content of the thought and the mental images in which it is embodied. It is because these mental images are the products of my body that the intellectual thought is my thought. This answer seems unsatisfactory for many reasons. Wittgenstein, who reawoke philosophers to the importance of the question of individuating the possessor of a thought, was surely better inspired when he urged us to look at the expression of a thought to supply the criteria for individuating its possessor. Aquinas has nothing of value to offer in the search for such criteria: his significance for the modern reader here is that he alerts one to the existence of the problem (*Aquinas*, p. 94).

Herbert McCabe protested against this passage. The account which I rejected, he said, was indeed unsatisfactory; but it had been rejected even more forthrightly by Aquinas himself in his *De Unitate Intellectus* when he dismissed the Averroist account of human thought. Averroes, Aquinas says, held the receptive intellect to be a substance quite separate from any human being; an intelligible species was the form and act of this intellect, but it had two subjects, or possessors, namely the receptive intellect and the phantasm of an individual human. Thus, the receptive intellect is linked to us by its form by means of the phantasms; so that when the receptive intellect understands, an individual human being understands. But this account, says Aquinas, is empty: '*Quod autem hoc nihil sit, patet*' (*De Unitate Intellectus*, ed. Keeler, Rome, 1936 sections 63–4).

Of the three reasons which Aquinas gives to prove the futility of the Averroist position, the following is the most persuasive. It is true, Aquinas says, that one item may have more than one subject or possessor: a wall's looking red to me may be the very same event as my seeing the redness of the wall. So there is no objection in principle to the idea that a species may be both a form of the receptive intellect and something which belongs to the phantasms. But that would not make the human being, whose phantasms these are, be an intelligent subject.

The link between the receptive intellect and the human being, who is the possessor of the phantasms whose species are in the receptive intellect, is the same as the link between the coloured wall and the faculty of sight which has an impression of that colour. But the wall does not see, but is seen; it would follow therefore that the human being is not the thinker, but that its phantasms are thought of by the receptive intellect (*De Unitate Intellectus*, section 65).

The positive account which Aquinas sets against the Averroist account is that the thoughts I think are *my* thoughts because the soul which thinks them is the form of *my* body.

McCabe is perfectly correct that this is Aquinas' official position. However, it seems that what Aquinas says elsewhere prevents him giving a convincing answer to the question, 'What makes my thoughts *my* thoughts?' He maintains that the soul can exist, and think, without the body. But, given the general Aristotelian hylomorphic theory to which he is committed, if X is the form of Y, then operations of X are operations of Y. Of course Aquinas denies that thinking is the operation of any bodily organ, and in that he is correct, if we are thinking of organs in the sense in which the eye is the organ of sight. But though thinking is not the operation of any bodily organ, it is the activity of a body, namely the thinking human being. That is to say, the manifestations, expressions, of my thoughts are the movements of my body, just as in general the manifestation of my knowledge of a language such as English consists in the movements of my speaking lips, my reading eyes, my writing fingers, my acting limbs. Hence it is not enough to say that my thoughts are *my* thoughts because the soul which thinks them is the form of my body: it is necessary to spell out the way in which it is my body which expresses the thoughts if the thoughts expressed are to be my thoughts.

But are there not unexpressed thoughts, the thoughts which pass through our minds in private, unvoiced thinking? Indeed there are, and we may well ask: what is it that makes these thoughts my thoughts? It may seem unhelpful, though it is true, to reply: they are thoughts which, if they were to be expressed, would be expressed by me. To make this answer seem less vacuous, and to convince ourselves that even in this case the criterion for the possessor is still bodily, we should reflect on cases of alleged telepathy or thought reading.

Suppose that at a thought-reading session, or seance, the thought reader or medium says, 'Someone in this room is thinking of Eustace.' Here, *ex hypothesi*, the occurrence of the thought has been ascertained through means other than normal bodily communication. Even here, the way we would seek to decide whether what the thought reader claimed was *true* would involve appeal to bodily criteria. What settles the matter is whose hand goes up, whose voice confesses to the private thought. And *whose* the hand is, *whose* the voice is, is determined by looking to see which body is involved.

Let there be no misunderstanding here. It is not being suggested that it is by observing actual or conjecturing hypothetical movements of my own body that I decide which thoughts are my own thoughts. Aquinas is indeed right that we 'perceive', that is to say know without any intermediary, what we are thinking. There is no state of mind in which I know that certain thoughts are present, and wonder whose thoughts they are, mine or someone else's. It is not by bodily criteria that I know which thoughts are mine, or know what I am thinking, because it is not by any criteria at all that I know these matters. But what it is that I know, when I know that certain thoughts are mine, is the same thing as other people know; and what I know, and what they know, is something to which the bodily criteria are necessarily relevant.

To sum up, then, the residual, unresolved, difficulty which vitiates Aquinas' account of self-knowledge. It is correct, as Aquinas says often (e.g., Ia 75, 6) that my thoughts are my thoughts because they are operations of the form of my body. But the only account which he gives of the way in which my body is involved in the operation of the intellect is his account of the way in which the phantasms are involved in our present life, at every level, in the exercise of thought. It is only by reifying the intellect, by treating form as something separable from matter, that he is able to avoid the Averroist account of the relation between intellect and imagination which, as he rightly says, is sheer nothingness.

5

Philosophy of Mind in the
Thirteenth Century

When our President did me the honour to invite me to introduce this plenary session on Thirteenth Century Latin Philosophy he invited me explicitly to approach the subject from the viewpoint of analytic philosophy.

My lecture will be analytic in both its method and its topic. It is a commonplace among both the practitioners and the critics of analytic philosophy that it is non-systematic. It attempts to deal with problems piecemeal rather than to construct an elegant and self-contained system. My paper, similarly, will not attempt a grand overview of the thirteenth century in Latin philosophy. To give such an overview would indeed be a super-human task. Instead I shall single out a particular theme – that of the philosophy of mind – and I shall single out two authors: Thomas Aquinas and Duns Scotus. By doing so, however, I hope to illustrate the wealth and diversity in the area of philosophical anthropology within the Latin thirteenth century.

Among philosophers in the Anglo-American tradition there has grown up, in the years since the second world war, a branch of philosophy, a philosophic discipline, which is sometimes called philosophical psychology and sometimes philosophy of mind. The existence of the subject as a separate discipline in recent times is due primarily to the influence of Wittgenstein and secondarily to that of Ryle. In other philosophical traditions since the Renaissance it is not so easy to identify, as a specific area of philosophical study, the field which bears the name 'philosophy of mind'. This is because since the time of Descartes the philosophical study of the operation of the human mind has taken place in the context of epistemology, the discipline which is concerned above all with the justification of our cognition, the vindication of claims to knowledge, the quest for reliable methods of achieving truth. Epistemology, as contrasted with philosophy of mind, is a normative rather than a descriptive or analytic branch of philosophy.

Naturally, the concerns which go under the name of philosophy of mind have not been absent from the syllabus of philosophy in the continental tradition. The description of mental states and processes and activities is, or should be, a necessary prerequisite for the evaluation, defence or criticism of them. But the special concerns and emphases of philosophy of mind have not been so clearly isolated from their epistemological settings even in the work of those philosophers that explicitly set out to do so, such as Brentano and Husserl. (In this as in other matters, Frege stands apart in a world of his own, being both continental and analytical at the same time.)

It was because of their radical anti-Cartesian stance that Wittgenstein and Ryle cleared the ground for analytical philosophy of mind. The anti-Cartesian stance was explicit, indeed blatant, in Ryle; it was tacit, but more profound, in Wittgenstein. The birth of analytical philosophy of mind was in fact a rebirth. For if we return behind Descartes, to the middle ages, we find that philosophy of mind and epistemology are no less distinct than in the tradition stemming from Wittgenstein. Medieval philosophical disciplines, one might say, are distinguished primarily on the basis of the texts of Aristotle which lie behind them. In this way the *De Anima* is the medieval text in philosophy of mind just as the *Posterior Analytics* is the medieval text on epistemology, to the extent that the subject of epistemology can be clearly identified in advance of the Cartesian programme. But of course since the greatest medieval philosophers were theologians first and philosophers second, it is to their theological treatises rather than to their commentaries on *De Anima* that one turns for their insights into philosophy of mind. I refer to the treatises rather to demarcate the subject than as the source of the remarks – which in any case will be of very great generality – which I am about to make.

Philosophy of mind concerns, one might say, the mind and heart of man – the cognitive and affective faculties of the human person, the intellect and the will, the senses and the feelings, the imagination and the emotions. In this lecture I want to draw a contrast between the way in which philosophy of mind, and in particular the philosophy of the intellect and the will, was treated by the two greatest philosophers of the thirteenth century, Thomas Aquinas and Duns Scotus. For these two thinkers, close though they stand to each other in time, are, as I shall hope to show, at opposite poles on the topics which nowadays belong to philosophy of mind. Recent developments in analytic philosophy reinforce, rather than diminish, the contrast between Aquinas and Scotus which has always been drawn by writers in the scholastic tradition. My conclusions will not be at all new, but will be perhaps reached from a novel direction.

It is, of course not only *within* the area of philosophy of mind that Scotus is very different from Aquinas; while Aquinas looks back to the Aristotelian tradition which separated philosophy of mind from epistemology, Scotus sets the fuse to the Cartesian explosion whose fall-out is with us to this day in the work of philosophers and psychologists.

I shall present the contrast between Aquinas and Scotus in two stages. First I shall treat of the cognitive side of the mind, the intellect – the relationship of the mind to truth – and secondly, the affective side of the mind, the will – the relationship of the human personality to goodness.

The contrast on the intellectual side is best approached through a consideration of Aquinas' doctrine of intentionality. Aquinas' theory of intentionality is an answer to the problem of the relation between the world and thought; the question, what makes a thought of X a thought *of X*? It is to this question that Aquinas proposes as an answer, the theory of the immaterial intentional existence of form in the mind.[1]

According to Aquinas, when I think of redness, when makes my thought be a thought of redness is the form of redness. When I think of a horse, similarly, it is the form of horse which makes the thought be the thought of a horse and not of a cow. What makes the

[1] *S. Th.*, Ia, 14, 1; 56, 1 ad 3; 79, 3 and 6; Ia IIac, 50, 4.

thought of a horse the thought of a horse is the same thing as makes
a real horse into a horse: namely, the form of horse. The form
exists, individualized and enmattered, in the real horse; it exists,
immaterial and universal, in my mind. In the one case it has *esse
naturale*, existence in nature; in the mind it has a different kind of
existence, *esse intentionale*, and indeed a special kind of *esse
intentionale*, immaterial existence. Aquinas' theory is a development
of the Aristotelian theorem of the identity in act of cognition and
what is cognized. This theory is easiest to grasp in the case of
sensation, sense-cognition. *Sensus in actu est sensible in actu*, as the
medieval Aristotelian slogan had it.

Let me illustrate what I take to be the meaning of this slogan
with the example of taste. A piece of sugar, something which can be
tasted, is a sensible object; my ability to taste is a sensitive potency;
and the operation of the sense of taste upon the sensible object is
the same thing as the action of the sensible object upon my sense;
that is to say, the sugar's tasting sweet to me is one and the same
event as my tasting the sweetness of the sugar. The sugar is actually
sweet, but until put into the mouth is only potentially tasting sweet:
that is to say, sugar outside the mouth is sweet 'in first act' but not
'in second act'. It is the second actuality, sweetness in second act,
which is at one and the same time the sugar's tasting sweet and my
tasting of the sweetness of the sugar. (Something like black coffee of
course is sweet neither in first act nor in second act, but only in
potentiality, in that you can make it sweet by putting sugar into it.)

Aquinas adopted this theory, and he frequently quotes the
Aristotelian slogan in its Latin version: *sensible in actu est sensus in
actu*. But he also emphasizes the corresponding doctrine about
thought as well as the theorem about sensation. Not only is the
actualization of a sensible object the same thing as the actualization
of the sense-faculty; so too the actualization of an object of thought
is the same thing as the actualization of the capacity for thinking.
Intelligibile in actu est intellectus in actu.[2]

With all respect to Father Lonergan, whose book *Verbum*[3] first
made me see the importance of these matters, I think that the
identity of the object of intellection in act with the intellect itself in

[2] *S. Th.*, Ia, 14, 2; 55, 1 ad 2.
[3] B. Lonergan, S. J., *Verbum: Word and Idea in Aquinas*, Notre Dame, 1967.

act is every bit as real an identity as the corresponding doctrine
about sensation. Lonergan, it is well known, denies this. Let me
explain what I think Aquinas' theory involves.

The object of thought exists, intentionally, in the intellect; its
existence is the actualization, the life, of the intellect. Intentional
existence and immaterial existence are not the same thing. A
pattern exists, naturally and materially, in a coloured object; it
exists, intentionally and materially, in the eye or, according to
Aquinas, in the lucid medium. The Archangel Gabriel is a form
which exists immaterially and naturally in its own right; it exists
immaterially and intentionally in Raphael's thought of Gabriel.
The characteristic of intellectual thought, whether of men or of
angels, is that it is the existence of form in a mode which is both
intentional and immaterial.[4]

Aquinas, I have said, against Lonergan, is committed to the
identity of the objects of thought and the activity of the thinker just
as he is to the identity of the activity of a sense-object and the
activity of the sense-faculty. But there is no doubt that the doctrine
about thought is more difficult to understand than the doctrine
about sensation. In stating the theorem of the identity in act of
knower and known, with regard to the senses, I said that a piece of
sugar was a sensible object. This is not strictly correct: it is the
piece of sugar *qua* sweet (*dulce*, 'the sweet') which is the sensible
object; it is the sweetness of the sugar whose actuality is identical
with the taster's testing, not the sugar itself. In the case of
something like sweetness, a secondary quality, it is easy enough, I
think, to accept the theorem of identity in second act. We can
understand that the secondary quality in act is one and the same as
the activity of the appropriate sense; the sweetness of X just is the
ability of X to taste sweet. (Of course it is related to various
chemical properties and constituents of X; but that relation is a
contingent one). But suppose that I think of the redness of X or the
sweetness of X: can it be said that those properties of X just are the
ability that X has to be thought of in that way? Surely not. So how
can the doctrine of identity in act apply to thought as well as to
sensation?

To see how, we have to recall that for Aquinas the real object of

[4] *S. Th.*, Ia, 56, 2 ad 3.

all human knowledge is form. The senses perceive the accidental forms of objects that are appropriate to each modality: with our eyes we see the colours and shapes of objects; with our noses we perceive their smells; colours, shapes and smells are accidental forms or accidents, as opposed to substantial forms, the forms which locate things in their appropriate species. The accidental forms which are perceived by the senses are individual forms not universals – it is the colour of *this rose* which I see – one cannot smell the universal *sulphur*. Substantial form, on the other hand, is grasped not by the senses but by the intellect: the proper object of the human intellect is the nature or form of material things. Material things are composed of matter and form, and the individuality of a parcel of matter is not something that can be grasped by the intellect. The intellect can grasp what makes Socrates a man, but not what makes him Socrates; it can grasp his form but not his matter; or, more strictly, it grasps his nature by grasping the form plus the fact that the form must be embodied in some matter or other of the right kind. But because it is matter which is the principle of individuation, the form which is grasped by the intellect is universal, unlike the individual accidental forms which are the objects of sense-perception.

Both thoughts and forms in the world are, in a sense, individual, but it is in a different sense in each case. The occurrence of redness in a particular rose is an individual occurrence because it is an occurrence of redness in a particular rose: it is the redness of *this rose*. But the occurrence of redness when Plato thinks of redness is not individual by being the thought of the redness of any particular thing, but by being a thought thought by a particular thinker, namely Plato. It was a constant doctrine of Aquinas that thought, as such, is not directly of individual things at all, neither of individual forms like the redness of Socrates nor of individual substances like Socrates himself.[5]

When I think of Socrates there is no form of Socrateity having intentional existence in my mind. Unlike Scotus, Aquinas would have denied that there was any such form to be in my mind. When I think of Socrates there is in my mind only the universal form of humanity; I can of course think of Socrates but to think of Socrates

[5] *S. Th.*, Ia, 86, 1; *De Ver.*, 2, 6.

I have to place this universal form within a context of sensory imagery (*phantasmata*). The individual humanity of Socrates has *esse naturale* in Socrates but it does not have *esse intentionale* in my mind or in anyone's mind; the universal, humanity, has *esse intentionale* in my mind, but it does not have *esse naturale* in Socrates or in any human being or anywhere in the world.

An adequate account of Aquinas' theory of knowledge and theory of intentionality has to give full weight to his thesis that there is no intellectual knowledge of individuals. In a famous passage Aquinas wrote:

> Plato thought that the forms of natural things existed apart without matter and were therefore thinkable; because what makes something actually thinkable (*actu intelligibile*) is its being non-material. These he called ideas. Corporeal matter, he thought, takes the form it does by sharing in these, so that individuals by this sharing belong in their natural kinds and types; and it is by sharing in them that our understanding takes the forms that it does of knowledge of the different kinds the types. But Aristotle did not think that the forms of natural things existed independently of matter, and forms existing in matter are not actually thinkable.[6]

Forms existing in matter, Aquinas says, are only thinkable in the same way as colours are visible in the dark. Colours are perceptible by the sense of sight; but in the dark colours are only potentially perceptible, not actually perceptible. The sense of vision is only actuated – a man only sees the colours – when light is present to render them actually perceptible. Similarly, Aquinas says, the things in the physical world are only potentially thinkable or intelligible. An animal with the same senses as ours perceives and deals with the same material objects as we do; but he cannot have intellectual thoughts about them – he cannot, for instance, have a scientific understanding of their nature. To explain our ability to do so we have to postulate a species-specific capacity for abstract thought: what Aquinas calls the agent intellect, the *intellectus agens*, which he contrasts with the receptive intellect or *intellectus possibilis*.

[6] *S. Th.*, Ia, 19, 3.

We, because we can abstract ideas from the material conditions of the natural world, are able not just to perceive but to think about and understand the world.[7]

Does this mean that Aquinas is an idealist? Does he mean that we can never really know or understand the world itself, but only our own immaterial, abstract, universal ideas? Aquinas was not a representative idealist: he explicitly rejected the thesis that the intellect can know nothing but its own ideas.[8] But Aquinas' thesis does mean that he is anti-realist in one of the many senses of that term. Though he did not think that we could know nothing but our own ideas, he did think that our knowledge of material objects could never be something which was purely intellectual. Contrariwise, our intellect is not directly capable of knowing anything which is not universal.

If Plato was wrong, as Aquinas thought he was, then there is not, outside the mind, any such thing as human nature as such; there is only the human nature of individual human beings such as Jack and Jill. But because the humanity of individuals is form embedded in matter, it is not something which can, as such, be the object of intellectual thought. In Aquinas' terminology, an individual's humanity is *intelligibile* (because a form) but not *actu intelligibile* (because existing in matter).[9] It is the agent intellect which, on the basis of our experience of individual human beings, creates the intellectual object, humanity as such. This, then, is the sense in which Aquinas, though not an idealist, is not a realist either. The ideas are not intermediate entities which represent the world: they are modifications of our intellect consisting in the acquired ability to think certain thoughts. But the universals which ideas are ideas of are themselves things which have no existence outside the mind, as universals. Their only existence, the only existence of these universals, is their ability to occur in thoughts. Thus the actuality of the universal thoughts is one and the same thing as the actuality of the capacity for intellectual thought; the actualization of the universals the only existence they have, the actualization of the intellect, the life of the mind – these two things are one and the same. *Intelligibile in actu est intellectus in actu.*

[7] *S. Th.*, Ia, 79, 3.
[8] *S. Th.*, Ia, 85, 2.
[9] *S. Th.*, Ia, 79, 3.

The theorem that the activity of a sensible property is identical with the activity of a sense-faculty, the *sensus in actu est sensibile in actu*, seems to be something which is strictly true only of secondary qualities like taste and colour; it is only of these that we can say that their only actualization, the only exercise of their powers, is the actualization of sense-faculties. A primary quality, like heaviness, can be actualized not only by causing a feeling of heaviness in a lifter, but in other ways such as by falling, by exerting pressure on inanimate objects.

But the intellectual theorem, *intellectus in actu est intelligibile in actu*, seems to me something which is still defensible as a formulation of a particular kind of anti-realism. (Whether it is ultimately defensible, I do not know.) The actuality of the power of the object of thought is the same thing as the actuality of the power of thinking. That is to say, on the one hand, the intellect just is the capacity for intellectual thought, the locus of thought; the intellect has no structure or matter; it is just the capacity for thought. On the other hand, the object of intellectual thought, humanity as such, is something which has no existence outside thought. Or so we must say unless we are prepared to embrace the Platonism which Aquinas rejected.

Of course material objects in the world are not to be identified with universals. They are objects which are thinkable in potency: their thinkability, their intelligibility, is simply their capacity to be brought under the universal concepts which are the intellect's creation.

Let us now contrast this position of Aquinas very briefly with corresponding positions in Duns Scotus. For Scotus there exists an individual essence for each substance which is an object of knowledge: the *haecceitas* of Scotist tradition. The *haecceitas* is a form, and therefore it can be present in the intellect. Because each thing has within it a formal, intelligible principle, the ground is cut beneath the basis on which Aquinas rests the need for species-specific *intellectus agens* in human beings.[10]

Individuals, unlike universals, are things which come into and go out of existence. If the proper objects of the intellect include not only universals but individuals – even individual forms like a

[10] *Opus Oxon.*, II, 3, 4, 3; I, 3, 2, 27; *Quodl.*, 6, 3.

haecceitas – then there is a possibility of such an object being in the intellect and not existing in reality (one and the same object being in the intellect and not existing in reality) – the possibility which Aquinas' intentionality theory was careful to avoid. An individual form may exist in the mind and yet the corresponding individual not exist. Hence the individual form present in the intellect can be only a representation of, and not identical with, the whose knowledge it embodies. Hence a window is opened, at the level of the highest intellectual knowledge, a window to permit the entry of the epistemological problems which have been familiar to us since Descartes.

In Aquinas' account no such window exists because there is nothing in the mind which the mind has not itself created. Of course, like all philosophers, Aquinas has to deal with problems of error in the sense perception, but the way in which this problem presents itself to him is a question of describing and accounting for the malfunctioning of a faculty. It is not a question of building a bridge between a correctly functioning faculty, or a correctly functioning cognitive apparatus, and an extramental reality. But that is what, through Scotus, and often in Descartes, the epistemological problem more and more explicitly became.

The differences between Aquinas and Scotus, so far as concerns the intellect, are not so much a matter of explicit rejection by Scotus of positions taken up by Aquinas. It is rather that a consideration of the Scotist position leads one to reflect on its incompatibility at a deep level with the Thomist anthropology.

But when we turn from the intellect to the will – from the mind to the heart – things are very different. Here Scotus is consciously rejecting the tradition which precedes him, he is innovating in full self-awareness. He regards Aquinas as having misrepresented the nature of the freedom of the human will considered in itself, and also as having misrepresented the relation between intellect and will.

Consequently, in the shorter second half of my paper I will reverse the historical order and instead of putting forward first Aquinas' account and then making a brief comparison with Scotus, I will put forward Scotus' account and make a brief comparison with Aquinas.

Duns Scotus is well known in the history of philosophy as being a voluntarist. What does this mean precisely? Scotus asks whether anything other than the will effectively causes the act of willing in the will.[11] He replies, nothing other than the will is the total cause of the volition of the will. What is contingent must come from an undetermined cause which can only be the will itself, and he argues against the position which he attributes to 'an older doctor', that the indetermination of the will is the result of an indetermination on the part of the intellect.

> You say: this indetermination is on the part of the intellect, in so representing the object to the will, as it will be, or will not be. To the contrary: the intellect cannot determine the will indifferently to either of contradictories (for instance, this will be or will not be), expect by demonstrating one, and constructing a paralogism or a sophistical syllogism regarding the other, so that in drawing the conclusion it is deceived. Therefore, if that contingency by which this can be or not be was from the intellect, dictating in this way by means of opposite conclusions, then nothing would happen contingently by the will of God or by God, because He does not construct paralogism nor is he deceived. But this is false.

Scotus' criticism of the idea that the indeterminism of the will arises from an indeterminism in the intellect is based on a misunderstanding of the theory that he is attacking. The intellect in dictating to the reason does not say, 'this will be' or 'this will not be', but rather 'this is to be' or 'this is not to be', 'this is good' or 'this is not good'. And, if it is the non-necessarily related means to good which is in question, it is possible for an intellect to dictate both that something is good and that the opposite is good. Moreover, Scotus' own theory, as well as having been based on a misunderstanding of the theory which he is attacking, led, as the later history of philosophy was to show, to an account of the freedom of the will which cannot avoid the problem of an infinite regress in the location of the indeterminate cause.

This is not a danger of which Scotus was unaware and in the

---

[11] *Opus Oxon.*, II, 25.

course of his discussion of divine foreknowledge of future contingents he introduces a new kind of potentiality which is
particularly involved in the freedom of the will.[12] When we have a
case of free action, Scotus wrote, this freedom is accompanied by an
obvious power to opposites, *una potentia ad opposita manifesta*. Because
though the will can have no power to will and not will at the same
time – that would be nonsense – there is in the will a power to will
after not willing, or to a succession of opposite acts. That is to say
that while A is willing X at time t, A can not will X at time t + 1.
This, he says, is the *manifesta potentia*, the obvious power to do a
different kind of act at a later time.

But, Scotus says, there is another, not obvious, power which is
without any temporal succession: *tamen est et alia, non ita manifesta,
absque omni successione*. That is a kind of power that he illustrates by
imagining a case in which a created will existed only for a single
instant. In that instant it could only have a single volition, but even
that volition would not be necessary, but be free. The lack of
succession involved in this kind of freedom is most obvious in the
case of the imagined momentary will, but it is in fact there all the
time. That is, that while A is willing X at t, not only does A have
the power to not will X at t + 1, but also the power to not will X at
t, at that very moment. This is Scotus' very explicit innovation, the
discovery of this non-manifest power. Many critics of Scotus from
Ockham onwards have agreed that it was a non-manifest power; a
power so non-manifest in fact as to be inconceivable. But it is
something which Scotus distinguishes carefully from logical possibility; it accompanies logical possibility, he says. It is not simply
the fact that there would be no contradiction in A's not willing X at
this very moment, it is something over and above – a real active
power – and it is the heart of human freedom.

Simo Knuuttila, in his rich and remarkable article *Time and
Modality in Scholasticism*,[13] has emphasized the importance of this
innovation in Scotus. He thinks that Scotus' presentation of this
new kind of power – a power to do the opposite of what you are
doing at the very moment when you are doing it – is in fact the
entrance into philosophy of the notion of alternative possible

[12] *Lectura*, I, 39, 1–5, n. 48–50.
[13] In S. Knuuttila (ed.). *Reforging the Great Chain of Being*. Dordrecht, 1981.

worlds, a notion which is one that is particularly thriving in certain analytical quarters at the moment.

Prior to Scotus, Knuuttila says, from Aristotle to the late thirteenth century, modal notions, like possibility and necessity, are in the last analysis reducible to temporal notions: what is possible is what is so at some time or other, what is necessary is what is so always; a necessary sentence is true whenever it is uttered, a possible sentence is at least sometimes true. All possibilities, therefore, are actualized in one and the same historical world: there is not room for possible worlds other than the actual world. It follows that, for every moment of time, what *can* then be actual *is* actual.

This pre-Scotus view is called by Knuuttila (following Hintikka) the statistical interpretation of modality. Knuuttila then goes on:

It seems that Duns Scotus played an important role in creating principles of modal thought, which are no longer bound to the limitation of the statistical interpretation of modality. In his modal theory, the meaning of modal notions is connected with the idea of considering different alternative states of affairs at the same time. In Duns Scotus' modal theory, the domain of possibility is accepted as an *a priori* area of conceptual consistency. It is then divided into different classes of conpossible states of affairs of which the actual world is one. Of logical possibilities (*possibile logicum*) some are real alternatives to the actual world (*possibile reale*). Such a possibility is characterized by the fact that it could be actual without any change in the general structure and general laws of the actual world. Thus it was not Leibniz who invented the idea of possible worlds, which has similarities with the contemporary understanding of modality as it is codified in the so-called possible world semantics. The basic idea is present in Duns Scotus' modal theory.[14]

I agree with Knuuttila that on this point Scotus is a great innovator, but I disagree with him on two points. First of all, I

[14] Ibid. p. 236.

disagree with him about the nature of the innovation and, secondly, I disagree with the implicit value judgement that the innovation was a beneficial one. I disagree with him that before Scotus the dominant, or the exclusive, understanding of possibility was a statistical one; that is, that possibility was reducible to truth at some other time.

In Aquinas' theory, if I have read him correctly, truth at a different time is not offered as an analysis of a statement that something is possible, it is rather offered as a criterion for it. (I am using the notion of criterion in the Wittgensteinian sense where a criterion for something is logically necessarily evidence for something but is not equivalent to it.) Secondly, while there is an undeniable similarity between Duns Scotus' theory and possible world semantics, I disagree in regarding the introduction of possible world semantics as a benefit to metaphysics. I think that possible world semantics has a number of uses in logic but that the metaphysical applications which have been made of it have led to a great deal of confusion. This is something that I only have time to state and not to argue here.

I turn back from Scotus to Aquinas. In Aquinas' theory of the will, the will is not, as with Scotus, a sovereign which is autonomous with respect to other faculties. Indeed, the will derives its very freedom from its intimate relationship to the reason and its dependence on the reason, on the intellect as capacity for practical reasoning. It is precisely because practical reasoning has a certain nature that the will is free. Practical reason is essentially defeasible: it cannot be apodictic like theoretical reasoning; and the reason for this is that the means to achieve the goals sought by the will are not necessarily connected with those goals in the way in which conclusions of theoretical reasoning are connected with the principles on which theoretical reasoning rests. And it is because of the defeasible nature of practical reasoning that the will, which is the capacity for rational choice, is itself free; that is, can opt between genuine alternatives.

Aquinas knows nothing of the 'non-manifest' power which Scotus regards as the key to the sovereignty of the will; nor does his system include the self-originating, self-determining acts of the will which give rise to the regress which, in later centuries of philosophical and theological debate, was to bring the very notion of the will into such philosophical disrepute.

I have presented two contrasts in philosophy of mind between Aquinas and Scotus, emphasizing in the one case the teaching of Aquinas and in the other the teaching of Scotus: the denial of intellectual knowledge of the individual in Aquinas, and the half-explicit acceptance of it in Scotus: the assertion of the autonomy of the will in respect to the intellect in Scotus, and the rejection of this in Aquinas. In each case the contrast in philosophy of mind, the contrast in philosophical anthropology, is accompanied by a contrast in metaphysics: the acceptance of the so-called *haecceitas* by Scotus in the one case, and his invention of a radically new type of possibility in the other case.

So in each case the contrast in philosophy of mind is based on, connected with, a metaphysical contrast, and the two metaphysical contrasts are related. If I am right, in each case Scotus is in the wrong and Aquinas is in the right, and in each case Scotus' metaphysical errors are a violation of the principle that there is no individuation without actualization. Let me say in conclusion just a few words about that principle. There is a converse principle, that there can be no actualization without individuation, that is, there are no actual universals. That principle – *no actualization without individuation* – would, I think, be very widely held by philosophers except those who are quite explicitly Platonists. But the converse principle – *no individuation without actualization* – is, in my view, an equally important metaphysical principle. Both these principles were, I believe, held by Aquinas, though many of Aquinas' followers would certainly reject the second. Belief in other possible worlds and belief that there are individuated substances which are not actual is in breach of this principle and, from the point of view of that principle, it matters little whether they are identical with or merely counterparts of individuals in this world. Individuation in possible worlds is always by description (not by acquaintance) and as there is no theoretical limit to the number of things which may actualize a particular description, violation of the principle that there is no individuation without actualization leads to philosophical confusion. If there is a *haecceitas* or an individual essence, a set of attributes which is metaphysically linked to an individual, then two things are possible; first, the intellect can know this and can know the individual, and secondly there can be full individuation in possible worlds other than our own. That is the way in which the two errors, as I believe them to be, are mingled together. In each case the metaphysical and epistemological consequences of the differences between Aquinas and Scotus are great and lie behind arguments which are today still very active. According to which side of the twentieth-century debate one takes, one will regard Duns Scotus as the first discoverer of hitherto obscure truths or as the originator of a mighty system of thought which has clouded our minds ever since. In either case the achievement, whether benign or malign, is a mark of the very great genius of the Franciscan doctor.

In philosophy it is the small differences which are the great ones and the differences which separate Aquinas and Scotus are, from the point of view of metaphysics and philosophy of mind, greater than those which separate the pair of them from Descartes and Leibniz. That is what makes the thirteenth century such an exciting one in the history of philosophy.

6

Wyclif: a Master Mind

The description of Wyclif as a Master Mind, I have discovered, causes many an eyebrow to raise in incredulity. In earlier centuries there would have seemed nothing more natural than to single out Wyclif in this way. Two famous encomia may be cited in illustration. John Milton, urging Parliament to innovative legislation on divorce, said this: 'It would not be the first, or second time, since our ancient Druides left off their pagan rites, that England hath had this honour vouchsaft from Heav'n, to give out reformation to the World ... Who but Alcuin and Wicklef our country men opened the eyes of Europe, the one in arts, the other in religion.' And in *Areopagitica*, arguing against prelatical censorship, Milton glories that out of England, as out of Sion, there were proclaimed and sounded forth the first tidings and trumpets of reformation to all Europe: 'And had it not bin the obstinat perversnes of our Prelats against the divine and admirable spirit of Wicklef, to suppresse him as a schismatic and innovator, perhaps neither the Bohemian Husse and Jerom, no nor the name of Luther, or of Calvin had bin ever known: the glory of reforming all our neighbours had bin completely ours.'

In the nineteenth century, Wyclif was honoured not only in the vanguard of the Reformers, but also as a pioneer of English literature. Ford Madox Brown, celebrating the flowering of the English language, matched his painting of Chaucer reading to the court of Edward III with a resplendent canvas of Wyclif reading his translation of the New Testament of John of Gaunt. Chaucer and Gower look on in admiration as Wyclif holds forth. Masterly indeed must be the mind of one who was both Morning Star of the Reformation and Founding Father of English Prose.

Wyclif's fame, however, rested on unstable foundations. The attribution of the English Bible was already questioned in the nineteenth century. Today the great majority of those who are in a position to judge believes that Wyclif had no more personal hand in the Wyclif bible than King James had in the King James bible. Equally, those who have studied most closely the surviving Wycliffite tracts hesitate to attribute any of them to the Reformer himself. Indeed, they doubt whether anything in English survives from his hand save a few fragments.

Wyclif's reputation, therefore, must now rest on his Latin writings and these are not easy to evaluate. In general one must say that those who admire Wyclif have not read his works, and those who have read his works do not admire them. Let us quote, for instance, the words of Lane Poole, who edited Wyclif's main work of political theory, *De Civili Dominio*:

> [Wyclif's] characteristics are what we expect in the age not only of *infima Latinitas*, but also of the extreme debasement of the scholastic method, when logic had ceased to act as a stimulus to the intellectual powers and had become a mere clog upon their exercise, and when men on longer framed syllogisms to develop their thoughts, but argued first and thought, if at all, afterwards (WS 1885, p. 66).[1]

The problem with Wyclif's Latin works is simple. In the nineteenth and most of the twentieth century, few outside a devoted band of Roman Catholic scholars read, or understood, medieval scholastic philosophy. Those Protestants who admired Wyclif as a Reformer neither understood nor cared about his philosophical system: scholasticism was part of the Romish darkness which the light of the Reformation had put to flight. Catholics who understood scholasticism paid little heed to Wyclif. Why study the texts of a worthless heretic when there were holy men of genius still awaiting editors?

[1] WS = Wyclif Society – Wyclif's Latin Works (London, 1882–1924)

If we are to reassess Wyclif we must take him from the Reformation pantheon and replace him in his Oxford context. There he can be understood by comparison with other Oxford reformers.

In the remarkable but neglected book *Enthusiasm*, (Oxford, 1948) Ronald Knox begins his life of Wesley thus:

> The biography of John Wesley is surely unique. Here is a man born in the first decade of his century, who sees it through into the last; a man so far in reaction from the tendencies of his age that he seems a living commentary on them, yet so much the child of his age that you cannot think of him as fitting in with any other. A High Churchman in his youth, he makes for himself in the unsympathetic surroundings of Oxford an enclave of primitive observance and of ascetic living; such is his personal influence that he seems destined, if that were possible, to shake Oxford out of its long dream. *Dis aliter visum*; he undergoes an experience of conversion before his lifetime has reached its mid-point. A sensational conversion; the finished product of the schools becomes the disciple of a foreign visitor to our shores, by no means his match in intellect. Thenceforward, he must fight by other methods, and for the most part with other companions, that battle against irreligion to which he has dedicated his youth. He has made his own soul, but the battle is not yet over; he finds himself in conflict with the men who had been his closest comrades in arms, and who still share his own beliefs but exaggerate their emphasis in a degree which he thinks dangerous. A man who once seemed likely to do great things for the Church of England, yet whose influence, on the whole, was to damage her position in the eyes in his contemporaries; a man, nevertheless, who lived to see something of the old bitterness against him die down, whose age was cheered by public recognition at once welcome, unsought, and unexpected.

So far, however, there is nothing unique about Joan Wesley. A careful reperusal of the foregoing paragraph will show that it all applied to the career of Cardinal Newman (p. 66).

Though Mgr Knox did not notice it, the common pattern which he traces between the lives of Wesley and Newman is a pattern which fits not only the eighteenth and the nineteenth centuries, but also the fourteenth: in each of the centuries the most important event in the religious history of Oxford was the defection of a favourite son from the religious establishment. To be sure, Wyclif did not live from the first to the last decade of the century; he was born in the twenties and died in the eighties of the fourteenth century. But like Wesley and Newman he was a fine flower of the Oxford schools, a man who stood out among his contemporaries for learning and austerity of life. Like them, he formed around himself a group of disciples, and seemed likely to dominate, by his personal influence and reputation, the course of the University's thought and practice. Like them, he took a doctrinal step which alienated his closest theological allies and vindicated the suspicions of his critics. Exiled from Oxford as they were exiled, he carried on his religious mission elsewhere, tireless in preaching, writing and controversy, casting only a rare nostalgic glance at the distant spires of the home of his youth and promise.

Newman and Wesley, Knox tells us, where both in youth High Churchmen. The term, applied to Wyclif, would make no sense; but there is no doubt that in his youth Wyclif was a philosophical and theological conservative. In philosophy he defended the good old cause of realism against the modernism of the nominalists. His enemies were philosophers such as Ockham who denied the reality of universals, stressed an empiricist theory of knowledge, and endeavoured to interpret metaphysical truths as truths of language. Before ever Wyclif appealed to the Bible to overturn the doctrines of the Popes, he was reminding Oxford of its very earliest days, when Grosseteste was its first chancellor, and he was appealing behind the scholastics of recent generations to the overarching authority of Augustine.

Mgr Ronald Knox applies to Wesley and Newman a description which would apply equally well to Wyclif: 'a man so far in reaction from the tendencies of his age that he seems a living commentary on them, yet so much the child of his age that you cannot think of him as fitting in with any other.' Wyclif stands out from later reformers by the profundity of his immersion in scholasticism; he

stands out from other scholastics by his position at the break-up of
the international academic scholastic community and the beginning
of the separate vernacular cultures. In this way he is totally a man
of one age: yet, like Wesley and Newman, he continued to speak to
generations yet unborn.

When he came to Oxford in the 1350s Oxford University had
been for more than a century one of the great centres of European
thought: it was just entering on a new period of comparative
independence and isolation from its great sister university at Paris.
The best known scholars of the generation before Wyclif, Duns
Scotus and William Ockham, were both well known in Paris as well
as in Oxford, and had lived long periods on the Continent; Wyclif
remained in England except for a brief visit abroad. University
lectures and sermons continued to be in Latin, and almost all
Wyclif's unquestioned works were written in that tongue; but
Oxford men now began to write and preach in English too.

The story of Wyclif's life is soon told: his history is essentially a
history of ideas. Though from time to time distracted by public
service – at one time engaged on an embassy, at another offering an
expert opinion to Parliament – he spent his life mainly in teaching,
preaching and writing. The history of his life is the list of the books
he wrote and the tale of the reactions of his readers. Between 1360,
when he was Master of Balliol, and 1372 when he took his DD, he
produced a philosophical *summa* whose most important volume is a
treatise on universals, designed to vindicate realism against the
criticism of the nominalists. In his maturity he wrote a theological
summa which began with two books of banal orthodoxy, moved
through several of hardy innovation, passed into overt heresy, and
ended in barren polemic. The volumes of this work covered the
whole range of medieval theology: three dealt with various forms of
Law (*De dominio divino*, *De mandatis divinis* and *De dominio civili*); this
last proposed the controversial theses of the disendowment of evil
clergy and the necessity of Christian communism. The *De Veritate
Sacrae Scripturae* was a treatise of biblical criticism, hailed by later
Protestants as an enunciation of the principle of *Scriptura sola*. In the
De Ecclesia, *De Officio Regis* and *De Potestate Papae* Wyclif analysed
the structure of Christian church and society, castigated abuses,
proposed reforms. In the *De Eucharistia* he discussed the Mass, the

centre of medieval spirituality. The hardihood of his speculations here, and in subsequent works, led to the condemnation of his teaching by an Oxford university commission. He retired to his county living at Lutterworth and continued writing, in increasingly strident tones of polemic, until his death in 1384. Though various councils had condemned propositions taken from his work, he died himself at peace with the church and his bones were allowed to rest – for a while – in consecrated ground.

In a lecture such as this there is not time for even the barest summary of Wyclif's thought. Instead, I shall try to illustrate the quality of his intellect by introducing three topics which are treated in his writings. The first will be drawn from philosophy, the second from natural theology, and the third from revealed, and in particular sacramental, theology. From philosophy I shall consider his argument in favour of universals against his nominalist adversaries. From natural theology, I shall consider his treatment of the problem of freedom and necessity: one of considerable importance give his posthumous reputation as a thoroughgoing determinist. From sacramental theology I shall take, from his discussion of the eucharist, his argument against the prevailing theory that in the sacrament the accidents remain without a substance.

First, then, realism and nominalism. Realism, for Wyclif, is above all a theory about the nature of universals; and the key to the understanding of universals is a grasp of the nature of predication. The most obvious form of predication is that in which subject and predicate are linguistic items, parts of sentences. The first philosophical sense which Wyclif attributes to the verb '*predicare*' or 'predicate' is 'the predication of one term of another'. 'This', he says, 'is the sense much talked about by modern writers, who think that there is no other' (*U*, I, 33). But in fact, he says, this kind of predication is modelled on a different kind of predication, real predication, which is 'being shared by or said of many things in common' (*U*, I, 35).[2]

Real predication, then, is not a relationship between two terms,

[2] *U* = *De Universalibus*, ed. I. J. Mueller, trans. A. Kenny (Oxford, O.U.P. 1985.) References are to the chapter and line number (which are the same in both Latin and English texts).

two bits of language. It is a relationship between the things in the world to which the linguistic items correspond. In a sentence such as 'Banquo lives' it is not the relationship between the subject-term 'Banquo' and the predicate-term 'lives', but the relationship between what the term 'Banquo' stands for, namely Banquo, and what it is in the world which corresponds to the term 'lives'. But what *is* the extra-mental entity which corresponds to 'lives'? Indeed *is* there anything in the world which corresponds to predicates? Wyclif's answer to the second question is that if not, then there is no difference between true and false sentences. His answer to the first question is his theory of universals.

A correct understanding of predication, Wyclif maintains, will enable us to see how far preferable a realist definition of universals is to a nominalist one. A realist will tell us simply that a genus is something which is predicated of many things which are different in species. A nominalist has to entangle himself in some circumlocution such as this: 'A genus is a term which is predicable, or whose counterpart is predicable, of many terms which signify things which are specifically distinct.' He cannot say that it is essential to a term to be actually predicated: perhaps there is no one around to do any verbal predicating. He cannot say that any particular term – any particular sound or image or mark on paper – has to be predicable; most signs do not last long enough for multiple predication. That is why he has to speak of counterparts, other resembling signs. He cannot say that the term is predicated of terms differing in species: the *word* 'dog' does not differ in species from the *word* 'cat'; they are both English nouns on this page. So he has to say that the terms signify things that differ specifically. But of course in doing this he gives the game away: he is making specific difference something on the side of the things signified, not something belonging purely to the signs. So the nominalist's gobbledygook does not really help him at all.

The nominalist is not entitled to say that things belong to a species or differ in species; how could a thing belong to a sign? If the species which contain individuals really were signs, then

> any logician could make the whole world and any of its parts in a tiny tangible body; there would be no more difficulty in putting the entire corporeal world into a tiny spot on a piece of

paper than in putting anything else into it. And thus anything
could belong to the species of anything; a man could belong to
the species of donkey, simply through a change in the
signification of the terms. (*U*, I, 389–91)

But of course we cannot alter the species and genus of things by
fiat, as we can alter the meanings of words by convention. It is not
the possibility or the fact of assigning a word which causes
extramental things to resemble each other more or less; the specific
resemblance or difference between things is based essentially on the
constituents of things themselves. The predication or predicability
of signs is not the reason for the resemblances between extramental
things; it is the other way round.

Wyclif's realism is not a mere logical thesis, and his devotion to
universals sometimes takes an almost mystical tone. He is prepared
to go so far as to say that all actual sin is caused by the lack of an
ordered love of universals: because sin consists in preferring lesser
good to greater good and in general the more universal good is the
greater good. Thus nominalism leads to selfishness, charity
demands realism.

I turn to my second illustration: the relation between freedom
and necessity. At the Council of Constance, after his death, Wyclif
was condemned for holding that all things happen by absolute
necessity, and he later had the reputation of being a crude
determinist. In fact, at least in his youth, Wyclif developed a
doctrine on this topic which was extremely subtle and nuanced. He
distinguished between no less than eight different types of
necessity, and he insisted that there were human actions which
were free in the sense of being exempt from any of these eight types
of necessity. (The eight types of necessity can be crudely catalogued
as: logical necessity, natural necessity, eternal truth, sempiternal
truth, inevitable truth, immutable truth, duress, and irresistible
impulse.)

Wyclif puts his distinctions to work in dealing with the paradox
of divine foreknowledge and human freedom. He puts to himself
the following paralogism:

It is necessary that particular events come about by absolute
necessity, for God necessarily and independently fore-ordains,

foresees, and wills, by the will of his good pleasure, every
particular creature. Nothing can resist his will, and so nothing
can prevent any effect. Just as no one can prevent the world's
having been, no one can prevent any effect coming to be at the
appropriate time. For the following argument is valid: God
ordains this; therefore this will necessarily come to pass at the
appropriate time. The antecedent is outside any created
power and is accordingly altogether unpreventable. Therefore, so is everything which formally follows from it (*U*, XIV,
294–305).

In the face of this objection, Wyclif reaffirms the crucial importance
of human freedom: not just freedom from compulsion, but genuine
freedom to choose between different alternatives. 'Many effects are
within rational creatures' free power between alternatives, in such
a way that they can make them to be and make them not to be;
otherwise merit and demerit would be eliminated' (*U*, XIV,
322–7). How are we to reconcile this with the divine control over
human actions? Wyclif's proposed solution is that we should say
that the relationship between the divine volition and the human
action is a two-way one: if God's volition causes man's act, so, in a
sense, man's act causes God's volition. It is in the power of man to
bring about, in respect of any of the eternal volitions in God, that
none of them will be, and similarly with his non-volitions and *vice
versa*.

> On this it is to be noted that the volition of God, with respect
> to the existence of a creature, can be understood as a
> relationship, a mental entity with its basis in God's willing the
> thing to be according to its mental being – which is something
> absolutely necessary – and with its terminus in the existence of
> the creature in its own kind. And such a relationship depends
> on each of the terms, since if God is to will that Peter or some
> other creature should be it is requisite that it should in fact be.
> And thus the existence of the creature, even though it is
> temporal, causes in God an eternal mental relationship, which
> is always in process of being caused, and yet is always
> completely caused. Nor does it follow from this that God is

changeable, since such a relationship is not the terminus of
any change . . . nor does it follow from this that man can
perfect God, or compel him, or cause in him volition,
knowledge, or anything absolute (*U*, XIV, 328–44).

Thus, when God wills Peter to repent of his sin, it is true to say both
that Peter is repenting because God wills him to repent, and that
God wills him to repent because he is repenting. But God's eternal
volition is a complex one, which includes other elements which in
no way depend on Peter.

So the proposition 'God wills Peter to grieve' reports many
volitions in God, for instance, the volition by which he wills to
be what is absolutely necessary, the volition by which he wills
the specific nature to be, and this depends on no particular
man, and the volition by which it pleases God that Peter
grieves, which is one that depends on Peter's grief (*U*, XIV,
346–52).

In this way the objection that if God's ordaining is outside our
power, then all that follows from his ordaining is outside our power,
is answered in a dramatic fashion. Wyclif simply denies the
antecedent: God's ordaining is not outside our power. God's
eternal volition, he says, 'is not completely caused before the
termination of the effect, although it is determinately and non-
disjunctively true'.

Does this mean that when I prevent something happening I
prevent God from willing? That would be absurd. 'When I prevent
a creature I do not prevent God from willing, since according to his
decree from all eternity he never willed the prevented creature so to
act.' But it is true that this eternal willing of God's is something that
I bring about (*U*, XIV, 386–99).

There is no necessary principle to the effect that if I can prevent
an antecedent from coming to pass, I can prevent a consequent
from coming to pass. What is true is rather that if the antecedent is
something altogether outside my power, to bring about or bring
about its contradictory, then anything logically following from it is
equally firmly so.

Wyclif sums up the relations between necessity and contingency:

All future things will come to pass necessarily by hypothetical necessity, and yet will come to pass most contingently. Similarly, the truths which thus necessitate them came to pass necessarily, and yet it can be the case that they did not. Indeed you can make it be the case that they did not, and yet you cannot make them cease to be, nor can you make what has been begotten not have been begotten . . . All these and similar things are obvious from the infallible principle that with God all things which ever have been or will ever be are present, and thus, if something has been or will be, it is at the appropriate time. Blessed, then, be the Lord of time, who has lifted us above time to see that magnificent truth (*U*, XIV, 409–24).

We can see, then, how misleading it is to suggest that Wyclif went beyond contemporary theologians in limiting human freedom in the interests of divine omnipotence. On the contrary, he took the highly unusual step of safeguarding human freedom by extending its sphere of action to the eternal voilitions of God himself.

It cannot be claimed that Wyclif's solution resolves the problem. When he distinguishes God's decrees into complex relational volitions, one simply wants to restate the objection in terms of the absolute mental volitions which are one element of the complex, an element which seems quite beyond human control. But no other medieval theologian succeeded in giving a satisfactory answer to the antinomy of divine power and human freedom, and perhaps no satisfactory answer will ever be possible. Where Wyclif departs from his colleagues is not in imputing extra necessity to human actions, but in assigning unusual contingency to divine volitions.

In theology Wyclif is best known for his attacks on the Papacy. But it was not Wyclif's views on the Papacy which led to his final breach with the teaching authority of the Church. It was when he turned his attention to the sacrament of the Eucharist, and gave an account of it which conflicted with the orthodox understanding of its nature, that he began to stand out in clear view as a heretic. When he denounced the Popes and questioned the validity of Papal claims he could find sympathizers even among the higher clergy; when he called for the disendowment of the Church, many laymen and begging friars found his words congenial; but when he attacked the doctrine of transubstantiation, friars, noblemen and bishops all turned against him, and the University which had hitherto sheltered him could no longer hold him. Events were to take a similar course nationally in the Reformation of the sixteenth century: bishops who went along with Henry VIII quite cheerfully when he threw off allegiance to the Pope and despoiled abbeys and priories were prepared, in the days of his son, to go to prison rather than accept any meddling with the Mass.

For most of his life, Wyclif accepted the traditional doctrine of the Eucharist; and he never ceased to venerate as a great sacrament the rite instituted by Jesus when at his last supper he took bread and said, 'This is my body', and took wine and said, 'This is my blood'. When, probably in 1379, he began to give the lectures which caused such a sensation, it was not the doctrine of the Real Presence that he was attacking, but the doctrine of transubstantiation as currently explained. The two doctrines are often confused by those unfamiliar with Catholic theology, but they must be carefully kept distinct by anyone who wishes to understand Wyclif. We may ask two questions about the Eucharist. First, do the words 'This is my body', uttered by Christ or his priest, make the body of Christ really, and not just symbolically, present? If you answer 'yes' to the question, then you believe in the doctrine of the Real Presence. We may then go on to ask: what then happens to the bread? Is it still there? To accept the doctrine of transubstantiation you have to give a negative answer: it is no longer there; it has been turned into the body of Christ.

It was common to all the standard accounts of the Eucharist that the accidents remained without a substance; they were not accidents inhering in the bread, for the bread was no longer there; nor were they accidents of the body of Christ, otherwise that would be small and white and round like the sacramental host. It is this theory of accidents without a substance which Wyclif regarded as quintessentially absurd, and he devises argument after argument to bring out the absurdity.

To talk of accidents without a substance is self-contradictory. Every accident which formally inheres in a substance is

nothing other than the truth that the substance is such-and-
such in an accidental manner; but there cannot be such a
truth without a substance, any more than there can be a
creature without God; so there is no such thing as a heap of
accidents without a subject which is the consecrated host (WS
1892, 63).

Any whiteness must be the whiteness of something; but the
whiteness of X is simply the truth that X is white; just as you can't
have a truth which is just the predicate '. . . is white' without a
subject, so you can't have an accident without a substance.

If you believe in the possibility of accidents without substance,
Wyclif now argues, you have no reason to believe in the existence of
material substances at all.

On this theory no intellect or sense proves the existence of any
material substance; because no matter what sense experience
or cognition is present it is possible and consistent that the
whole created universe is just a ball of accidents; so someone
who wishes to posit material objects must rely on the faith of
Scripture (WS 1892, 78).

Believers in transubstantiation, then, are reduced to a position of
phenomenalism: the world may be nothing but experience, except
where Scripture tells us the contrary. But Scripture does not even
tell us of our own existence. No doubt each of us is self-conscious,
but that does not tell us that we have a body as well as a soul;
neither sense nor reason, if Wyclif's opponents are right, tell us we
exist.

So of each of us it should be piously doubted whether he
exists, and what he is. This would make it very difficult to
examine the work of the clergy, to count the number of monks
and to list the coins and gifts they have been given. Because
each person could be a spirit linked to bare accidents, in
which case he would not be the kind of man we know (WS
1892, 79).

But this whole theory turns God into a deceiver. The theologians postulate the continuance of the accidents, so as to avoid having to say that the senses are deceived; but if there is no bread and wine there, then our inner judgement is even more grievously deceived.

> Since the sense of men, both inner and outer, judge that what remains is bread and wine exactly like unconsecrated stuff, it seems that it is unworthy of the lord of truth to introduce such an illusion in his gracious giving of so worthy a gift (WS 1892, 57).

The philosophical reader of Wyclif cannot help but be reminded of Descartes by these passages. Descartes, like the opponent Wyclif sets up, thinks that all the deliverances of inner and outer senses are, in themselves, compatible with the non-existence of the external world. Only the veracity of God convinces us of the reality of body as well as mind. And human beings, as conceived by Descartes, really are spirits linked to bare accidents; for the only matter which he recognizes is bare extension.

These points of Wyclif are well taken: but he goes further in trying to convict his adversaries of absurdity. Those who say that they see Christ in the sacrament should tell us whether he is standing or sitting, and tell us what colour and size he is in the different hosts: is he lighter in one and darker in another, big in one and small in another? Must not Christ move in six different ways at once when four priests carry the host to four points of the compass, one lifts it up and another puts it down? These questions are unfair taunts, because it was not part of the theory of Wyclif's opponents that the accidents of the host inhered in the substance of Christ; it was precisely to avoid saying that the whiteness of the host was the whiteness of Christ that the theory of self-subsistent accidents was introduced. But, Wyclif says, if the link between Christ's body and the accidents of the host is broken, then how does the presence of the host on the altar effect the presence of Christ on the altar? For being in a place is an accident just as much as being white or being round or being an inch in diameter.

Wyclif's philosophical arguments against transubstantiation are powerful. But he is equally opposed to the doctrine on theological grounds: it is an unscriptual innovation. St Thomas Aquinas may have taught it, though it is more charitable to suppose that his works were tampered with by evil friars after his death. But if he did teach it, it was a rash doctrine to teach, and quite unproved.

It is rash, because it sets out as an article of faith that neither bread nor wine remains after the consecration; which is excessively rash for many reasons; for it is an article which occurs in none of the three creeds of the church. What plausibility is there in saying that because of the rash assertion of one man the Church is to be burdened with a new article of faith? (WS 1892, 140).

Wyclif's own view is that the bread remains after the consecration; the visible and tangible accidents, after as before, are accidents of the bread. None the less, it does truly become the body of Christ, and Wyclif uses a number of illustrations to show how this can come about.

When writers write letters, words and sentences the paper and ink remain beneath the symbols. But through custom and skill those who can read pay much more attention to the significance of the symbols than to the natural characteristics of the signs to which an illiterate would attend. Much more so the habit of faith brings the faithful to grasp through the consecrated bread the true body of Christ (WS 1892, 144).

The afterlife of Wyclif is as interesting as his life. When we turn to his influence after his death, the first topic to consider is Bible translation. Clearly, whether or not he himself translated, he was anxious for the Bible to be put into the vernacular. I quote an ancient translation of the *De Officio Pastorali*:

The Holy Gost gaf to the apostles wit at Witsunday for to knowe al maner languages to teche the puple Goddes lawe therby; and so God wolde that the puple were taught Goddes lawe in diverse tunges; but what man on Goddes half shoulde reverse Goddes ordenaunce and his wille? And for this cause

Seynt Jerom travelede and translated the Bible fro diverse
tungs into Latyn that it myghte be after translated to othere
tunges. And thus Crist and his apostles taughten the puple in
that tunge that was most knowen to the puple; why shulden
not man do so now? And herefore autors of the newe law, that
weren apostles of Jesu Crist, writen their gospels in diverse
tunges that weren more knowen to the puple. Also the worthy
rewme of Fraunce, notwithstondynge all lettinges hath translated the Bible and the Gospels with othere trewe sentences of
doctours out of Latyn into Freynsch, why shulden not
Englishce men do so? As lordes of Englond han the Bible in
Freynsch, so it were not agen resoun that they hadden the
same sentence in Englishce; for thus Goddes law wold be
bettere knowen and more trowed for onehed of wit, and more
acord be betwixte rewnes (ch. XV).

Did Wyclif himself put these precepts into practice? The early
manuscripts of the English Bible do not bear his name, and
scholars nowadays are generally unconvinced the Wyclif wrote or
even supervised the two versions of the English Bible that have
come down to us from this period,[3] though they were undoubtedly
the work of men influenced and inspired by his teaching. In fact,
the evidence for Wyclif's own responsibility for Bible translation is
not negligible. The chronicler Henry Knighton, not long after his
death, wrote thus:

This master John Wyclif translated the gospel, which Christ
had entrusted to clerks and to the doctors of this church so
that they might minister it conveniently to the laity and to
meaner people according to the needs of the time and the
requirement of the listeners in their hunger of mind; and he
translated it from Latin into the English, not the angelic,
idiom (*In Anglicam linguam non angelicam*) so that by this means
that which was formerly familiar to learned clerks and to those
of good understanding has become common and open to the
laity, and even to those women who know how to read . . .

[3] See, for instance, Anne Hudson, 'Wyclif and the English Language' (in *Wyclif in his
Times*, ed. Kenny) from which the following quotation from Knighton is taken.

... a state of affairs which Knighton regarded as shocking. Knighton was writing about 1392, only ten year after the events which he claims to record; and he was a canon of the Augustinian house of Leicester, where one of his colleagues was Philip Repton, one of Wyclif's closest disciples. So he was in a position to know what he was writing about. Later, John Hus was to report that the English said that Wyclif had translated the whole Bible into English; and Archibishop Arundel, writing to Rome about his Constitutions of 1407 which forbade the making of new biblical versions, reported – in rather obscure language – that Wyclif had been responsible for making English versions of the sacred text.[4]

Wyclif's relation to the Wycliffite Bible is a topic on which I hesitate to express an opinion which goes against that of those who are much more qualified to judge than I am. It may be that there are linguistic arguments, drawn from the dialect and idiom of the versions, which make impossible the traditional ascription. This is a field in which I can only bow to those who are experts where I am ignorant. But so far as the purely historical argument runs, I must confess that it seems to me that it is as imprudent to assert that Wyclif had no hand in the Bible as it was to assert that he was its sole or major author. The evidence of Knighton is the evidence of a man who was in a position to know, and who had no particular motive for inventing the story. It dates from barely a decade after the events it purports to record. Many events in Wyclif's life are reported by scholars without embarrassment on the basis of much less contemporary evidence. It seems to me easier to explain away the absence of Wyclif's name from the manuscripts where it does not appear than to explain its presence in those where it does: after all, during much of the lifetime of our manuscripts it was a serious offence to possess or to read any Wyclif manuscript; and we know that Wyclif's Latin Bible commentary survived in the Bodleian only because his name was expunged from the manuscript and remained hidden until it was revealed by ultra-violet light in 1953.[5]

[4] Wilkins, Concilia Magnae Britanniae and Hiberniae, III, 350 (cited in Hudson, 'Wyclif and the English Language').

[5] See B. Smalley, 'John Wyclif's Postilla super totum Bibliam', *Bodleian Library Quarterly* 4 (1953), p. 188.

It has often been pointed out that in his few years at Lutterworth Wyclif could not have had time to write all the vernacular works attributed to him. But it seems to me equally implausible that a compulsive writer, driven from a place where Latin was the normal medium of communication to an arena where evangelism had to be in the vernacular, should have left it entirely to others to pursue this task.

What, next, of the influence of Wyclif's teaching? In England the Lollards, in Bohemia the Hussites kept green his memory. But what of the Universal Church of the fifteenth century? Here the matter was determined by the reaction of Christians to the Council of Constance.

During his lifetime Wyclif was never personally condemned as a heretic. A provincial synod at Blackfriars in 1382 had considered 24 propositions, concerning the Eucharist, the limits of clerical power, the dispensability of the Papacy, and the wrongness of clerical endowment; 10 of the propositions had been condemned as heretical and 14 as erroneous, but Wyclif had not been condemned by name. His retirement and subsequent death allowed the official proceedings to rest. It was not in England but in Bohemia that, in the early years of the fifteenth century, the debate on his doctrines was most fierce. In 1403 the 24 Blackfriars propositions were condemned in Prague, and 21 new theses were added to them, making a list of 45 errors. In 1409 Archbishop Arundel appointed a commission at Oxford to identify errors in Wyclif's works: they drew up a list of 267 suspect propositions for condemnation.

It was at the Council of Constance in 1415 that Wyclif's teaching was officially condemned by the Universal Church. The condemnation was delayed by nationalist rivalry. All wanted Wyclif condemned, but the German nation wanted the 45 Prague propositions damned, while the English wanted the 267 Oxford theses condemned. It was not until the fifteeth session, the one memorable for the execution of Jan Hus, that Wyclif was condemned. First the 45 propositions were proscribed; then 260 out of the 267. The 260 propositions were not read out in their entirety. The conciliar decree says that they had been examined, and it had been determined that some of them were notoriously heretical, and long condemned by the holy fathers; that some were blasphemous, others erroneous, others scandalous, some offensive to pious ears, and some rash and seditious. Not attempt was made to attach theological notes to particular theses. Only 58 were read out during the session. But all the articles were condemned. 'The sacred synod by an everlasting decree proscribes and condemns the aforesaid articles and any or each of them, forbidding each and every Catholic, under threat of anathema, to dare to preach, teach, put forward or maintain the said articles of any one of them.' Having condemned 305 Wycliffite propositions the Council proceeded to deal with Hus: he was condemned, handed over to the secular arm, and burned that same day.[6]

The condemnation of Hus has long been censured by Protestant writers as an example of cruel perfidy. But the condemnation of Wyclif, in the form it took, was itself outrageously unfair. Not that he was innocent of heresy, nor that a more careful judgement would have been unable to give a precise definition of the heresy. The point is that it was quite unjust to condemn, under a global anathema, propositions which many of the Council fathers themselves regarded as falling far short of heresy.

A good example of the influence which the Constance condemnations exercised on theology and philosophy can be seen in the University of Louvain during the half-century after its foundation in 1425. Here, a quarrel between the faculties of theology and arts, concerning the implications of the condemnation of Wyclif's doctrine of necessity, led to the development of a system of three-valued logic, and the eventual prohibition of that system by the Pope in 1474.[7]

As the fifteenth century drew to its end, Wycliffite ideas seemed dead in all the major centres of learning in Christendom. But in the second decade of the sixteenth, as new heresies set Europe ablaze, many thought they could recognize in the new figure of Luther the familiar lineaments of Wyclif.

When Lutheran heresy came to England, it was regarded by the orthodox as a revival of Wyclif's teaching. King Henry VIII, in a letter to Saxony, claimed that the errors of Luther were 'pure

---

[6] See A. Kenny, 'The Accursed Memory', in *Wyclif in his Times*, ed. Kenny, (Oxford, O.U.P. 1986).

[7] See L. Baudry, *La Querelle des Futius Contingents*, (Paris Uni, 1965).

Wyclifism'. In controversy with Tyndale, More described Wyclif as 'the first founder of that abominable heresye, that blasphemeth the blessed sacrament' and complains that Tyndale regarded Wyclif as a Jonah sent to warn Nineveh of its sins.[8]

On the Continent as well as in England Wyclif was regarded, by friend and foe alike, as a precursor of the Reformation. At Worms an edition of the *Trialogus* appeared in 1525, the first of Wyclif's works to be printed and the only genuine one until the nineteenth century. In 1528 a Wycliffite commentary on the Apocalypse was printed at Wittenberg with a preface by Luther. On the Catholic side, Bartolomeo Guidiccio, writing to Paul III in 1538 to urge the summoning of a general council to anathematize the errors of the reformers, drew up a list of twenty Lutheran propositions. Nine of these, he claimed, were old errors of Wyclif already condemned at the Council of Constance. But the Wycliffite propositions condemned at Constance had begun a new life of their own. A Protestant admirer published a set of 'aphorisms of John Wyclif'. They were none other than the condemned articles.

When the Council of Trent met to codify the Catholic position against the heresies of the Reformation, the anathemas laid upon Wyclif were frequently cited, especially in the Eucharistic session of 1547. One year later, on the Protestant side, John Bale, in his catalogue of British writers published at Basel, hailed Wyclif as 'the most strong Elias of his times' and wrote that 'he shone like the morning star in the midst of a cloud, and remained for many days as the faithful witness of the church'. John Foxe, in a Latin Protestant martyrology published at Strasbourg in 1554, gave Wyclif and his followers pride of place among the victims of tyrannical Roman persecution. This martyrology, after Foxe's return to England, grew into the *Acts and Monuments* which for ever canonized Wyclif's role as the great English precursor of the Reformation.[9]

Many English Catholic writers set out to refute Foxe. In Elizabeth's reign the most tireless critic of Wyclif was Nicholas

---

[8] *Complete Works of Sir Thomas More*, (New Haven, Yale University Press, 1963), VIII, p. 587.

[9] See M. Aston, 'John Wycliffe's Reformation Reputation,' *Past and Present* 30 (1965), pp. 21–31.

88 *Heritage of wisdom*

Harpsfield, Archdeacon of Canterbury in the days of Pole. In one of the dialogues he wrote in 1566, he says that Wyclif is an uncomfortable ally for the reformers: Wyclif approved of the worship of relics and images, for instance. Luther, he says, regarded Wyclif as a heretic; and he quotes Melanchthon, writing about the Lord's supper:

> I have looked at Wyclif, who makes a great stir on this issue, but I have found in him many other errors, which permit one to judge of his spirit. He did not understand or maintain justification by faith. He naively mixes up politics with the gospel, and did not realize that the gospel allows us to accept the lawful regimes of all nations. He claims that priests are not allowed to possess any private property, and thinks that tithes should be paid only to teachers . . .[10]

Setting Wyclif against the more recent reformers became a standard move of Counter-reformation apologetic.

Foxe, in later editions of his *Book of Martyrs*, replied to some of the taunts of the pseudonymous 'Cope', and some fifteen years later Harpsfield returned to the charge. In captivity he wrote a lengthy history of the English Church: to it he added a long appendix, a *Historia Wicleffiana*, a history of English heresy to match the history of English piety.[11] The history combines a chauvinistic pride in the extent of Wyclif's influence (a single Englishman filling the whole world with his ideas) with a horror at the wickedness of his heresy (no decent Englishman believed a word of Wyclif's teaching until the present pestiferous generation). Readers will find, says Harpsfield, that Luther borrowed not only his abuse of the Roman Church, but all his heresies, from Wyclif – except that on the issue of the Eucharist Wyclif is even worse than Luther. He matches Lutheran heresies against the articles condemned at the Council of Constance. But the latter-day disciples of Wyclif, he insists, disagree with their master about image-worship, celibacy and pacifism.

[10] *Dialogi Sex . . . ab Alano Copo*, N. Harpsfield (Antwerp, 1566).
[11] *Historia Anglicanae Ecclesiae* (Douai, 1622).

Better known than Harpsfield was the Jesuit Robert Persons, who drew on his work in his own *Treatise of Three Conversions of England* in 1603. His book was an elaborate reply to Foxe's *Book of Martyrs* and his heavily annotated copy can still be seen in the English college in Rome. Persons mocks at the calendar of Protestant martyrs in which Foxe places Wyclif at the head, as martyr of the day for January 2nd. Wyclf was no martyr, but died in his bed; and many of the doctrines he held would make a good Protestant blush. To be sure, Foxe had admitted that 'in John Wickliffe's opinions and assertions some blemishes perhaps may be noted: yet such blemishes they be, which rather declare him to be a man that might erre, than which directly did fight against Christ our Savior'. But this is not enough for Persons. Is it all right, then, to fight indirectly against Christ? It is evident, Persons says, from the articles alleged by Foxe that Wyclif held many points of the Catholic religion now disowned by Protestants, such as holy orders, consecration, excommunication, distinction of venial and mortal sins and the like. He concludes, sweepingly, 'Wickliffe, Husse, and other like sectarys did hold many more articles with us against the protestants, than with them against us' (*Treatise* 1, 486).

One of Persons' most interesting critics was Thomas James, the first librarian of the Bodleian library, who in 1608 wrote *An Apologie for John Wickliffe, showing his conformitie with the now Church of England.* He took as his target both ill-informed Protestants and ill-willing Papists. He announced that his intention was to reply to Wyclif's critics 'out of his own words and works as they are extant in sundray old manuscripts in our so renowned public library'. He takes the reader through a series of topics of Reformation controversy: the authority of Scripture, the role of vernacular translations, the authority of tradition, the claims of the Papacy, justification by faith, the doctrine of the Eucharist. He has little difficulty in showing that on most of these issues Wyclif's position was closer to that of the Church of England than to that of the Church of Rome. Scripture, for Wyclif, contains all that is necessary for a Christian, and should be available in the vernacular; tradition is subservient to Scripture, and the Pope's power is limited, and Popes should not meddle with the affairs of princes. The Church of Rome may err: 'Wickliffe remains, in this point, as

in all the former, a resolved, true Catholike English Protestant'
(*Apologie*, 2, 10, 145, 23).

What, then, finally, is the importance of Wyclif in an age of
ecumenical theology and analytical philosophy? We can answer
this question by returning to the paradox from which we began and
the ambiguities which we have discovered. Wyclif, we said, was
read by few of those who admired him, and admired by few of those
who had read him. Those who revered him as a reformer were
repelled by his scholasticism, and those who could stomach his
scholasticism were disgusted by his heresy. During the Reformation
period neither Catholic nor Protestant could, in good conscience,
claim him as an unambiguous ally.

But here lies the secret of Wyclif's contemporary interest.
Persons and James were both indeed correct in claiming that
Wyclif contained much that supported their own side in the
Reformation debate. Precisely because he was a thinker who
anticipated many Reformation insights while firmly enframed
within the Catholic tradition, his writings have much to offer those
who seek to combine the positive elements of both traditions while
discarding the negative and divisive elements. It is true that his
later works strike an unhelpful note of polemic, though he never, at
his worst, descends to the level of the fishwife Latin in which
Luther and More tangled with each other. But in his major
writings, up to and including the *De Potestate Papae* and the *De
Eucharistia*, there is much that can speak to both the contemporary
heirs both of the Church of England within which he worked and of
the Roman church which he tried to reform.

It could not be claimed that his political writings, in this century,
have anything to offer to anyone but the historian. No doubt if he
were to return to earth Wyclif would be surprised to find that of all
his ideas it was communism that had, in the long term, found the
greatest echo – though communism arrived at by reasoning very
different from his own, and imposed by methods very different from
his.

I, for my part, am neither a theologian nor a political theorist but
a philosopher: and I will end by saying why I find Wyclif's
philosophy a particularly exciting treasure house of ideas at the
present time. It is only in recent decades, for the very first time

since the Council of Constance, that it has become possible to read Wyclif with an unblinkered philosophical eye. This has come about because of the secularization of scholasticism.

Up to the time of the Second Vatican Council scholastic philosophy was above all the confessional philosophy of the Roman Catholic Church; all Catholic institutions of higher learning were obliged to teach scholasticsim, and hardly anyone not a Roman Catholic took any serious interest in the study of it. Thus Wyclif's philosophical writings were a closed book, eschewed by non-Catholics because of their scholasticism, and abhorred by Catholics because of the heresy into which their author fell.

In the last few decades, all that has changed. Since the Second Vatican Council Roman Catholic philosophers have become eclectic, and Roman Catholic theology is interpreted into thought systems very different from those of medieval scholasticism. Compensatingly, scholars of other religions and of no religion have begun to take a purely philosophical interest in medieval thinkers; not just in great theologians like Aquinas and Scotus, but also humbler logicians such as William of Sherwood and Walter Burley. The linguistic turn which Anglo-American philosophy has taken in the present century has made it easier to enter into the writings of thirteenth and fourteenth century semanticists whose philosophy, like current analytic philosophy, attached an overwhelming importance to the logical analysis of the forms of ordinary language. For the first time, then, philosophers today are in a position to read Wyclif's philosophy unfettered by confessional prejudice, and unhindered by lack of comprehension of scholastic questions and answers.

Wyclif was the last of the major scholastics. No later pre-Reformation writer has a comparable breadth of vision or sharpness of dialectical talent. To read him is an excitement because of the way in which he combines virtuosity in scholastic method, and indeed a conservative scholastic metaphysic, with a set of emphases and concerns which are manifestly continuous with those of the modern world of the Renaissance and the Reformation. It is still too early to make a considered judgement on his standing in the overall history of philosophy: his own works have not yet been sufficiently studied, nor are those of his predecessors sufficiently well known, for us to take the measure of the profundity and originality of his mind. But it may well be that when the scholarly accounts can at length be cast Wyclif will be seen to rank with Scotus and Ockham as a worthy member of a great Oxford triumvirate. As the light dies from the Morning Star of the Reformation, that of the Evening Star of Scholasticism may glow brighter and brighter.

7

The Realism of Wyclif's
De Universalibus

Wyclif has long been famous as a realist, but the precise content of his philosophical realism has never been exactly determined. Ivan Mueller's 1985 edition of the *De Universalibus* gives the general reader, for the first time, an opportunity to take the measure of Wyclif's theory. The present article aims to single out some of the main themes of Wyclif's realism and to make them intelligible to those more familiar with contemporary than with scholastic philosophy.

Realism, for Wyclif, is above all a theory about the nature of universals; and the key to the understanding of universals is a grasp of the nature of predication. Everyone is familiar with the division of sentences into subject and predicate: in the sentence 'Banquo lives', 'Banquo' is the subject and 'lives' is the predicate; so too 'dogs' is the subject and 'bark' the predicate in 'dogs bark', or so at least a medieval grammarian would have been likely to say. This distinction is a distinction between bits of language: we are talking about terms and sentences, not about anything which terms or sentences might mean or represent or stand for. The word 'Banquo' is the subject of the sentence 'Banquo lives': it is a particular part of that sentence. But what about the man Banquo? Is he the subject of the sentence too? Well, if he is – and there are a number of idioms which make it natural to say so – he is not any part of the sentence in the way that the word 'Banquo' is. Banquo is the extralinguistic item for which the word 'Banquo' stands; he is what the sentence

'Banquo lives' is about, but he is not anything which that sentence contains (as it contains the word 'Banquo').

Wyclif, like everybody else, recognizes as the most obvious form of predication that in which subject and predicate are linguistic items, parts of sentences. The first philosophical sense which he attributes to the verb '*predicare*' or 'predicate' is 'the predication of one term of another'. 'This', he says 'is the sense much talked about by modern writers, who think that there is no other.' (*U* I, 33.) But in fact, he says, this kind of predication is modelled on a different kind of predication, real predication, which is 'being shared by or said of many things in common' (*U* I, 35).

Real predication, then, is not a relationship between two terms, two bits of language. It is a relationship between the things in the world to which the linguistic items correspond. It is not the relationship between the subject-term 'Banquo' and the predicate-term 'lives', but the relationship between what the term 'Banquo' stands for, namely Banquo, and what it is in the world which corresponds to the term 'lives'. But what *is* the extramental entity which corresponds to 'lives'? Indeed *is* there anything in the world which corresponds to predicates? Wyclif's answer to the second question is that if not, then there is no difference between true and false sentences. His answer to the first question is his theory of universals.

Life is the universal which corresponds to the predicate 'lives'. It is life which is shared by or said of many things in common. (The use of 'said of' should not mislead one into thinking that life is a linguistic entity, like the word 'life'. That is not so, any more than the fact that Caesar is much spoken of means that Caesar is a piece of speech.) 'It is in this manner', Wyclif says, 'that every actual universal is predicated of its inferiors in nature.' (*U* I, 35.) Plants live and stones do not; plants are inferiors, and stones are not, of life, in the sense that plants *come under* life in a pyramid of classification of the things there are in the world, whereas stones do not come under that heading.

Wyclif's adversaries, the nominalists, deny that there is any such thing as real predication, anything in the world corresponding to the predicate of a true proposition. They object as follows: 'Nothing is a subject or a predicate unless it is a part of a proposition. But things in the external world are not parts of propositions; therefore they are not predicates or subjects. Consequently no real universal is predicated' (*U* I, 80).[1] But this objection, Wyclif retorts, depends on a misunderstanding of the nature of a proposition. Besides the written or spoken propositions, sentences which are linguistic entities, there are real propositions in the extralinguistic world. A real proposition is what a true sentence corresponds to, just as real predication corresponds to the predication of terms. Walter Burley is cited as authority for the thesis that 'the truth on the side of reality, which God puts together from subject and predicate, is the real proposition' (*U* I, 91).[2] Human beings put sentences together from verbal subjects and verbal predicates; it is God who puts together, from non-linguistic entities, the real proposition which makes the verbal sentence true.

If we look in modern philosophy for a terminology to correspond to the 'real proposition' of Burley and Wyclif, we find it in the *sachverhalt* of Husserl and the early Wittgenstein. The problems which arise from Wyclif's account of the real proposition are the same as those which arise from the theory of *sachverhalt* in the modern philosophers: what makes negative propositions true? What makes false propositions false? What makes the truth of true future and past-tensed propositions?

Wyclif adopts a number of traditional Aristotelian distinctions between types of predication. There is *per se* predication, as in 'Socrates is human', and *per accidens* predication as in 'Socrates is white'. Subdivisions of *per se* predication are quidditative predication (as 'Socrates is human' or 'Socrates is animal') and qualitative predication (as 'Socrates is rational'). *Per accidens* predication comes in nine types corresponding to the last nine of Aristotle's ten categories (*U* I, 40–74). For Wyclif, in all cases of real predication a subject *says* its predicate (thus 'each man *per se* says the specific human nature which is the quiddity of each man', *U* I, 44) and a predicate is *said of* its subject (thus 'white is said of man', *U* I, 67). It is thus that Wyclif interprets familiar passages of Aristotle.

---

[1] Sed obicitur contra illud per hoc quod nihil est praedicatum vel subiectum, nisi pars propositionis. Sed res extra non sunt partes propositionis. Igitur non sunt praedicata vel subiecta. Et per consequens nullum universale ex parte rei praedicatur.

[2] Veritas ex parte rei, quam Deus componit ex subiecto et praedicato, (est) realis propositio, ut ponit Magister Walterus Burleigh.

Thus, in the Categories, in the chapter on substance, he maintains that primary substance is not said or predicated of anything. But secondary substance, such as genera and species, is said or predicated of a subject, as will become clear. This is more easily understood about things signified than about their signs, and it is a sense of predication which must be carefully noted (*U* I, 150–5).[3]

All this, while controversial, covers familiar ground. Less commonplace is Wyclif's threefold classification of real predication (*U* I, 157–69).

We must note carefully the three different kinds of predication, namely formal predication, essential predication and habitudinal predication. All such predication is principally in the real world. And this is why philosophers do not speak of false predication of signs, nor of negative predication, nor of predication about the past or the future, because that is not in the real world; only true predication is in the real world, though truly in the real world one thing is denied or removed from another, as man from donkey and similarly with other negative truths. But only that which is form is really predicated of a subject.[4]

Wyclif's definition of formal predication is not altogether easy to understand, but the examples he gives to illustrate this kind of predication – such as 'man is an animal' and 'Peter is musical' – suggest that what he has in mind is the case where a predication is made true by the inherence of an appropriate form (whether substantial, as in the case of animality, or accidental, as in the case

[3] Ut in Praedicamentis, capitulo de substantia, ponit primam substantiam de nullo dici vel praedicari. Secundam vero substantiam, ut genera et species, dici vel praedicari de subjecto, ut patebit. Hoc melius intelligitur de signatis quam suis signis et iste sensus praedicationis cum diligentia est notandus. Cf. Aristotle, *Categories*, 5, 2a 13.

[4] Diligenter est notandum de triplici praedicandi manerie, scilicet de praedicatione formali, de praedicatione secundum essentiam et de praedicatione secundum habitudinem. Talis autem praedicatio principaliter est ex parte rei. Et hinc philosophi non loquuntur de falsa praedicatione signorum nec de praedicatione negativa, nec de praedicatione de praeterito vel de futuro, quia talis non est ex parte rei, sed solum vera praedicatio, licet vere ex parte rei una res negatur vel removeatur a reliqua, ut homo ab asino et sic de aliis veritatibus negativis. Solum autem illud quod est forma praedicatur realiter de subiecto.

of musicality) in a subject. Habitudinal predication, on the other hand, is not made true by the inherence of a form. The accidental form of size inhering in Socrates does not vary while, owing to the growth of Simmias, Socrates changes from being taller than to being smaller than Simmias. Similarly if Socrates is thought of by Wyclif, this does not, as such, involve any change taking place in Socrates. Habitudinal predication, Wyclif says, is 'where a relationship of a kind attaches to a subject without making it as such strictly speaking changeable. Thus a thing can be thought of or loved, can cause various effects, can acquire place and location in time and many kinds of notional relations without as such being changed or changeable' (*U* I, 235–46).[5]

But it is essential predication which is the hardest to understand, and the matter remains dark when Wyclif gives us the examples that are meant to illustrate what kind of thing he has in mind: 'God is man', 'Fire is water', 'The universal is particular'. It is clear from the context that, in terms of Wyclif's theology, physics and logic, each of these propositions is meant to be in some sense true.

Given the doctrine of the Incarnation, the theological example appears easier to understand than the others. Its truth clearly depends in some way on there being one person, Jesus, who is both God and man. But in fact Wyclif does not say this: he says that in essential predication the same *essence* is the subject and the predicate. And in the case of the physical example he explains that 'the same essence which is at one time fire is at another time water'. And to explain the logical example he says, 'in the same essence there inheres both being a man and being this man. And being a man is common to every man, and this is formally universal, while being this man is restricted individually to this essence' (*U* I, 195–217).[6] The notion of 'essence' involved here is obscure, and clearly different from the standard medieval scholastic one. Anyone who could clarify it would do a great service to Wyclif scholars.

---

[5] Tertia est praedicatio secundum habitudinem ex qua secundum genus adveniente subiecto non oportet ipsum ut sic esse proprie mobile, ut contingit rem intelligi, amari, varie causare et acquirere sibi ubicationem, quandalitatem et quotlibet relationes rationis, sine hoc quod ipsum ut sic moveatur vel sit mobile.

[6] Eidem essentiae inest esse hominem et esse istum hominem. Et esse hominem est commune omni homini et sic universale formaliter, sed isse istum hominem est individualiter appropriatum isti essentiae.

For Wyclif believes that the correct understanding of predication as he explains it will enable us to accept the realist definition of universals rather than the nominalist one. The realist definition of 'genus' is brief and clear: 'Genus is what is predicated quidditatively of many things which differ in species.' The genus of animal is not a word, or symbol, but a reality: it is what is common to each animal, and is what is predicated – really predicated – of each animal quidditatively. (Quidditative predication, as contrasted with qualitative predication, tells you what kind of thing something is, as opposed to what properties or qualities it has.) 'Not all modern logicians gathered together', says Wyclif, 'could improve a single word of the definition' (*U* I, 350).

The modern logicians, or nominalists, since they do not accept real predication but only the predication of terms, are forced into terrible mazes when they try to define genus. They offer something like the following: a genus is a term or concept which is predicable (or whose counterpart is predicable) *per se* in the nominative quidditatively of many terms which signify things specifically distinct (*U* I, 857–60).[7]

For the realist, genus is an extra-linguistic reality; for the nominalist it is a term, an element of language, or a concept, an element of thought. The realist can say that genus is predicated, whereas the nominalist can only say it is predicable. Dogs are always animals, whether or not anyone is thinking or talking of animals; but it is only when someone is thinking or talking of animals that the *term* 'animal' is predicated. Moreover, if you take a single term such as the sound 'animal' produced by me at this moment – and if you are a nominalist keen to keep your ontology down to empirical particulars this is the only kind of thing you have a right to be talking about – then it is not true that it is even predicable of all animals. The sound would not last long enough to form part of all the different true sentences which would attribute animality to the various kinds of animal. That is why the nominalists have to add the rider 'or whose counterpart is predicable'. Now it is essential to genus that it should be related to different species; it is essential to a nominalist definition of genus

---

[7] Genus est terminus vel conceptus qui – vel secum convertibilis – est per se praedicabilis in recto et in quid de multis terminis significantibus res distinctas specifice.

that this relationship should be a relationship to different terms, not different extramental realities. But the nominalist cannot say that the term is predicated of terms differing in species; the word 'dog' does not differ in species from the word 'cat'. So the nominalist has to say that the terms signify things that are specifically distinct. But in doing so he checkmates himself: he is making specific difference something on the side of the things signified, not something belonging purely to the signs. But that is realism, not nominalism (*U* I, 355, 371).

For a consistent nominalist, Wyclif insists, substances do not resemble or differ in species, nor do they belong to any species; there cannot be any such thing as a species except as the product of a mind. But signs and thoughts are human creations; words and terms can change their meaning at their users' whim. If species therefore were signs or thoughts, we could change the species of anything simply by taking thought. 'Thus any thing could belong to the species of anything; a man could belong to the species of donkey, simply through a change in the signification of terms.' (*U* I, 389–91.)

Nominalism, according to Wyclif, is a ridiculous attempt to put the cart before the horse.

> Neither the possibility nor the fact of assigning a term can cause extramental things to resemble each other more or less. The specific resemblance or difference between things is not the reason for the resemblance of extramental things; it is the other way round – in the first and principal place you have to look in the things themselves for the specific resemblances and differences, and only subsequently in the signs.[8] (*U* I, 425–30.)

The nominalist's attempt to give an account of meaning without universals collapses under its own weight, containing its own

---

[8] Cum nec impositio nec imponibilitas termini sit causa quare res extra magis aut minus conveniant – quod convenientia et differentia rerum fundantur essentialiter in rerum principiis et non in signis, ut praedicatio signorum vel eorum praedicabilitas non est causa convenientiae rerum exterarum sed econtra – oportet igitur scrutari in rebus ipsis convenientias et differentias specificas primo et principaliter, et consequenter in corum signis.

refutation. The existence of universals is established by the
refutation of the opposing view. But if there are universals, what
kind of thing are they? Can the realist be sure that his own position,
like that of the nominalist, will not turn out to be internally
incoherent? It is to these questions that Wyclif devotes the major
part of his treatise.

Drawing on Grosseteste's commentary on the *Posterior Analytics*,[9]
Wyclif explains that there are five types of universal.

The first and foremost kind is the eternal notion or exemplar
idea in God. The second kind is the common created notion in
the superior causes, like the intelligences and the heavenly
spheres. The third kind of universal is the common form
rooted in its individuals. This, says Grosseteste, is what
Aristotle's genera and species are. Fourthly, there is the
universal which is the common form in its accidents,
apprehended by the lowest form of intellect. There is a fifth
kind of universal – signs and mental acts – which Grosseteste
sets aside as irrelevant to his concerns[10] (*U* II, 165–77).

We may note in this fivefold scheme two points of agreement
between Wyclif and his adversaries. The fifth kind of universal is
one which nominalists and conceptualists accept: it is the only
created kind of universal they are prepared to admit. The
acceptance by Wyclif that the first and foremost kind of universal is
a notion in the mind of God goes some way to meeting the
conceptualists' claim that it is in the mind that universals have
their home: but of course these universals of the first kind are prior
to any human mind. From all eternity, in God's mind there is the
thought of all he will or can make: these are the patterns and
paradigms by which he creates, referred to by Wyclif, as by other
Latin theologians, under the Greek word 'Idea'.

[9] Robertus Grosseteste, *In Aristotelis Posteriorum Analyticorum Libros* (Venice, 1514; repr.
Minerva GmbH, Frankfurt, 1966), I, 7, f. 8v.

[10] Primum et supremum genus est ratio vel idea examplaris aeterna in Deo. Secundum
genus est ratio communis creata in causis superioribus ut intelligentiis et orbibus caelestibus.
Tertium genus universalium est forma communis fundata in suis individuis. Et illa, inquit
Lincolniensis, sunt genera et species de quibus loquitur Aristoteles. Quarto forma communis
in suis accidentibus, apprehensa ab intellectu infimo, est universale. Sed quintum modum
universalium – pro signis vel actibus intelligendi – dimittit Lincolniensis ut sibi impertinens.

The second kind of universal we may leave aside as being of interest only within the context of medieval Aristotelian cosmology. It is the third kind of universal over which the battle between realists and nominalists principally rages.

Unlike the divine Ideas, which exist eternally whether or not there is a created universe, the universals of this third kind are brought into existence by creation. These universals are the forms which are shared in common by all the individuals of a kind. This, Wyclif maintains, is what Aristotle meant by genera and species. Elsewhere he calls them metaphysical universals (U II, 245).

Metaphysical universals are all universals: they are themselves instances of the universal 'universal'. But this is something which it takes an abstractive intellect to grasp: a dog may perhaps have a grasp of caninity (in that it recognizes other dogs as beings of the same kind as itself) but it certainly cannot grasp that caninity is a universal. Hence, universals, considered as universals in relation to their contingent instantiations, have a universality which is introduced by the intellect. This appears to be what Wyclif means when he talks about the fourth kind of universal ('the common form in its accidents, apprehended by the lowest form of intellect'), which he elsewhere calls logical universals (U II, 245).

The fifth kind of universal, the kind accepted even by nominalists, might be called 'grammatical universals', though Wyclif does not seem to use exactly this expression. Logic, he says, is midway between grammar and metaphysics. Logic shares in the conditions of each, treating primarily of realities, since it is the route to metaphysics, and secondarily of signs, since it is the terminus of grammar (U II, 108–11). Thus the logical universals come between metaphysical universals and grammatical universals. To grasp the logical universal is to realize the link between the metaphysical, extralinguistic universal, and its conceptualization in language. Logical universals, unlike metaphysical universals, presuppose created minds (U II, 240–50).

In propounding this fivefold scheme Wyclif reveals himself as being a realist but not a Platonist. He is not a Platonist because he does not accept that there are any universals outside the divine mind which are independent both of the existence of individuals and of the existence of created minds. Metaphysical universals are independent of created minds, but they are not independent of the existence of individuals of particular kinds. Logical universals may be independent of the existence of individuals (such at least seems to be the case with the universal 'chimaera') but they are not independent of the existence of created minds. Because of these qualifications to his realism, Wyclif is able to present himself as being an orthodox Aristotelian.

It is true that there are many passages in Aristotle where universals are criticized, most famously the dictum of chapter fiften of the first book of the *Posterior Analytics*, which read, in the version known to Wyclif, 'goodbye to the universals, for they are monsters'.[11] But, Wyclif maintains, when Aristotle is attacking universals his target is never the metaphysical universals which are the third kind in the Grosseteste scheme. It is the ideal universals of the first class. Wyclif agrees that if such Ideas are regarded as self-subsistent substances, separate from God and from individuals, then they are superfluous monstrosities (*U* II, 197). But none of Aristotle's arguments, he claims, are successful against ideal universals considered as notions in the mind of God. Wyclif is not quite sure whether Plato's own theory involved the superfluous monstrosities Aristotle attacked, or whether Aristotle had got his master's doctrine wrong. Wyclif himself, of course, did not know Plato at first hand. 'But it seems to me more probable', he said, 'that Plato's view of ideas was sound and in accordance with our own sacred Scripture as Augustine testifies' (*U* II, 200–3).

On the positive side, Wyclif can pont to many passages in Aristotle which favour realism about metaphysical universals. One of the clearest occurs in the chapter on substance in the *Categories*, where the Philosopher says that primary substance is not said or predicted of anything, but that secondary substance, such as genera and species, is predicated.[12] This, Wyclif argues, must be understood as meaning real predication; and the substance which is thus predicated is universal, the common natures which make individuals the kinds of things they are.

Now are these metaphysical universals prior or posterior to the

[11] *Analytica Posteriora*, I 15, 83a 34–5.
[12] *Categories*, 5, 2a 13.

relevant individuals ('supposits')? Wyclif's answer contains a distinction that is not at first sight obvious.

> The universal of which Aristotle is speaking is the common nature rooted in its supposits. In this way, in the order of generation in which they cause the universals, the subjects come first. Universals, on the other hand, take precedence in the order of origin, in which, both formally and finally, they cause their supposits (*U* II, 235–40).[13]

What this seems to mean is this. There is no such thing as human nature until there are individual human beings: there is no Platonic Ideal Man outside the divine mind. In this sense the existence of human beings brings into existence the universal humanity. But when there are human beings it is their humanity which makes them human (causes them formally) and the point of the succession of human beings is the perpetuation of the human species (which therefore causes them finally).[14]

Such then, is broad outline, is Wyclif's theory of universals. How does he argue for its correctness? How does he argue for the existence of universals other than by criticizing nominalism?

The argument is essentially simple: Wyclif maintains that anyone who believes in objective truth is thereby already committed, whether they know it or not, to belief in real universals. The two beliefs are in fact two forms of the same belief: one a complex form and the other a non-complex form. If the only truths we knew were protocols of immediate experience, perhaps it would not be obvious that there must be universals; but for most of Wyclif's adversaries it is common ground that the mind knows at least some universal, abstract truths.

> Since, therefore, we have to grant that there is a universal abstract truth of this kind, beyond the scope of a material sense-faculty to know, it must be concluded that there is a supra-sensible faculty, a kind of intellect, to consider it. And

---

[13] Universale de quo loquitur Aristoteles, est natura communis fundata in suis suppositis. Et sic praecedunt subiecta in via generationis, quo causant universalia. Econtra autem universalia praecedunt in via originis, qua formaliter et finaliter causant sua supposita.

[14] This account seems to apply only to those universals which are natures, where we have a species propagated by natural generation.

this is what philosophers call the agent intellect. To conceive the universal intention by abstracting from the phantasm, as the intellect does, is to perceive that every man resembles every other in being a man. And once the intellect has abstracted an everlasting eternal truth of this kind from perishable particulars, it sets itself the task of conceiving, in a non-complex manner, the name of the universal, whether specific or generic (*U* III, 37–46).[15]

The point can be generalized. If the mind is aware that an individual A resembles an individual B, there must be some respect C in which A resembles B. But in seeing that A resembles B in respect C, the intellect is *eo ipso* seeing the C-ness of A and B; this is to say, it is conceiving C-ness, a universal common to A and B. Seeing that A is like B in respect of C is the very same thing as seeing the common C-ness; so what is indicated by the complex clause in the first expression must be the same as what is indicated by the abstract noun in the second. Universals, then, are just universal truths grasped in a non-complex manner, and anyone who can make judgements of likeness automatically knows what a universal is.

So someone who wants to be made acquainted with the quiddity of universals has to think confusedly and abstractly, by genus and species, of the same thing as he first thought of by means of a complex whose subject is the specific or generic term; thus the species of man is the same thing as there being a man, and the genus of animal is the same thing as being an animal. And each of these is common to its supposits (*U* III, 90–5).[16]

[15] Cum igitur sit dare talem veritatem universalem abstractam quam non est sensus materialis cognoscere, relinquitur quod sit dare virtutem supra sensum, ut puta intellectum, qui illam consideret. Et hoc est quod philosophi dicunt intellectum agentem. A phantasmatibus abstrahendo concipere intentionem universalem ut intellectus est percipere quod omnis homo convenit cum quolibet in esse hominem. Et postquam abstraxerit a singularibus corruptibilibus huiusmodi perpetuam veritatem, imponit sibi ut incomplexe concipitur nomen universalis vel speciei vel generis.

[16] Volens igitur manuduci in notitiam de quidditate universalium debet intelligere confuse et abstracte idem per genus et speciem quod intelligit primo per complexum, cuius subiectum est terminus specificus vel terminus generis, ut idem est species hominis et hominem esse, idem genus animalis et esse animal. Et utrumque illorum est commune suis suppositis.

For Wyclif it is not enough to criticize nominalists or to offer this proof of the reality of universals. It is necessary also to provide answers to the conundrums by which nominalists seek to impugn the coherence of real universals. If we postulate a common humanity, must we also postulate a common personality, since every man is a person; and if so, does that mean that the whole human race is one person? (*U* VIII, 8) If you postulate something common to two human beings, are you set off on an infinite regrees, like the one sketched by Plato's Third Man argument? (*U* IX, 9ff.) Can a universal be created or changed or brought into being in any way? (*U* XII, 145ff.) Can universals be annihilated? (*U* XIII, 3ff.)

Typical of the nominalist cavils which Wyclif has to answer is the following passage from the eleventh chapter of the treatise:

> The human species is the subject of its own species and of other accidents. So too, then, it is characterized by them, e.g. it is created, it moves from place to place, it is multiplied in quantity, and so on with each of the accidental predicates. But if you grant this, many absurdities follow, as that the same thing is black and white, hot and cold. And, briefly, whatever predicate inheres in any man, inheres in the species of man, so that in one place it is most virtuous and most beautiful, in another most vicious and monstrous; it has more heads than Argus, eats more than Milo, is more procreative than Priapus, and so on (*U* XI, 27–38).[17]

'Many people', Wyclif comments, 'bring up ridiculous points when they are short of arguments'. But he makes a patient attempt to answer the difficulties, and to show how non-absurd and non-arbitrary answers can be given to these and similar trick questions. In dealing with the paradoxes he makes great use of the notion of essential predication.

[17] Sicut igitur species humana subicitur proprio speciei et aliis accidentibus, sic denominatur eisdem, sicut creatur, movetur localiter, multiplicatur in quantitate et sic de quolibet praedicatis accidentibus. Sed, hoc dato, multiplicantur quotlibet inconvenientia, ut quod eadem res sit alba et nigra, calida et frigida. Et, breviter, quaecumque praedicatio inest alicui homini, inest speciei hominis, ut hic esset virtuosissima, pulcherrima, ibi viciosissima et monstrusissima, cum habet plura capita quam Argus, magis edula quam Milo, plus procretiva quam priapus, et sic de multis ridiculose adductis a pluribus quando eis deficiunt argumenta.

Wyclif's realism is not a mere logical thesis and his devotion to universals sometimes takes on an almost mystical tone. Thus in answer to the objection that universals are superfluous unless they do something in the world, he replies, 'It is clear, since universals regularly do what they ought to, that they do great service to their God, since he is Lord of them before he is Lord of individuals' (*U* XI, 230–2).[18] Moreover, Wyclif believes that error about the nature of universals leads to all kinds of moral error. Here he enlists the support of Augustine's *De Vera Religione*, ch. 9 (*Patrologia Latina* 34, 161).

What everyone must principally love in his neighbour is that he is a human being, and not that he is his own son, or someone useful; for according to Augustine it is being a man which is what is common and is in an especial manner the work of God, since it precedes every particular human being, while being your son, or your mistress, is something you have brought about yourself (*U* III, 115–20).[19]

Augustine may well be right that every Christian ought, as Wyclif says, to love his neighbour in his common nature and not primarily with an eye to private utility, kinship, or pleasure. But the argument that one should love the more universal rather than the more particular would lead to odd conclusions which Wyclif would surely not have accepted: for instance, that one should love one's fellows as fellow animals rather than as fellow men.

Wyclif is prepared to go so far as to say that all actual sin is caused by the lack of an ordered love of universals: because sin consists in preferring lesser good to greater good and in general the more universal good is the greater good.

Thus if proprietors who are devoted to particulars were more concerned that a well-ordered commonwealth should thrive,

[18] Cum universalia regulariter faciunt quod debent, patet quod multum deserviunt Deo suo, cum prius sit dominus eorum quam individuorum.
[19] Ut quilibet debet principaliter amare in proximo quod est homo et non quod est filius suus vel sibi utilis, quia esse hominem, secundum Agustinum, est commune et praecipue opus Dei, cum praecedit quemlibet hominem singularem. Sed esse filium tuum vel amicam tuam, hoc est opus tuum.

than that their kinsfolk should prosper, or their relations or the people linked to them by locality or some other individuating condition, then beyond doubt they would not press, in the disordered way they do, for their own people to be raised to wealth, office, prelacy and other dignities (*U* III, 152–8).[20]

In this passage we can see, in the young Wyclif, the logician linking hands with the reformer. Nominalism leads to selfishness, charity demands realism. 'Intellectual and emotional error about universals is the cause of all the sin that reigns in the world.' (*U* III, 162–5.) In the whole history of philosophy has realism ever had a more enthusiastic champion than Wyclif?

---

[20] Ut si proprietarii singularibus dediti plus appretiarentur quod res plublica vigeat ordinata, quam quod cognati vel affines sui vel quomodocumque ex loco vel alia conditione individuante confoederati promoveantur, tunc indubie non inordinate sic instarent ut sui sint exaltati ad divitas, officia, praelatias vel alias dignitates.

8

The Conscience of Sir Thomas More

Samuel Johnson said that Sir Thomas More was the person of the greatest virtue these islands ever produced. Robert Bolt took these words as an epigraph for his play, *A Man for All Seasons*. In the preface to the play he explains how he understands them: Thomas More was 'a man with an adamantine sense of his own self' – a man who knew how far he would yield to love and to fear, but who became rigorous and unyielding when at last 'he was asked to retreat from that final area where he located his self'. This theme is worked out skilfully as the play proceeds. First of all we see More surrounded by his household and honoured by King Henry VIII: a judge resisting bribes from litigants, a courtier resisting threats from Cardinal Wolsey. His household steward, who represents the Common Man in the play, laments his generosity. 'My master Thomas More would give anything to anyone. Some day someone's going to ask him for something that he wants to keep; and he'll be out of practice. There must be something that he wants to keep.'

We do not have to wait long to find out what this is. More becomes Lord Chancellor; and Henry seeks his approval for his divorce from Queen Catherine and his marriage with Anne Boleyn. More refuses. He cannot acquiesce with a clear conscience. His wife, sensing his danger, urges him to be ruled by the King. 'If you won't rule him,' she says, 'be ruled!' More replies: 'I neither could nor would rule my King. But there's a little . . little area . . . where I must rule myself. It's very little – less to him than a tennis court.' Later his friend, the Duke of Norfolk, urges him to give in. 'I can't give in; you might as well advise a man to change the colour of his eyes.' Norfolk appeals to their friendship: is the one fixed point in a world of changing friendships the fact that Thomas More will not give in? 'To me it has to be,' says More, 'for that's myself! Only God is love right through, and *that's* my *self*.'

After King Henry marries Anne Boleyn, an Act of Succession is passed which derogates from the authority of the Pope. More refuses to swear to the Act. As the ultimate upshot of this, he will be beheaded. He explains to his daughter why he refuses to swear. 'When a man takes an oath,' he says, 'he's holding his own self in his own hands. Like water; and if he opens his fingers then, he needn't hope to find himself again.' Finally More is tried for treason, because he refuses to accept Henry as supreme head of the Church of England. At the trial, he is confronted by Thomas Cromwell, the King's Machiavellian secretary, who is organizing his destruction. 'In matters of conscience,' says More, 'the loyal subject is more bounden to be loyal to his conscience than to any other thing.' 'And so provide a noble motive,' retorts Cromwell, 'for his frivolous self-conceit!' 'It is not so, Master Cromwell – very and pure necessity for respect of my own soul.' 'Your own self, you mean!' says Cromwell. 'Yes,' replies More, 'a man's soul is his self.' And a stage direction underlines the importance of this confrontation: 'They hate each other and each other's standpoint.'

Robert Bolt's play is historically accurate in many details; and it contains many of More's own written or recorded words, so people who see the play or the film may well believe that the historical More saw his own action in the light in which it is placed by the quotations I have given. I think this would be a great mistake; the real More would not have agreed that a man's soul is a self of the kind described by Robert Bolt. I will try to explain why.

When More was first shown the Act of Succession and asked to swear the oath, he wrote to his daughter recording the reply he had made to the royal commissioners:

> I shewed unto them that my purpose was not to put any fault either in the act or any man that made it, or in the oath or any man that sware it, nor to condemn the conscience of any other man. But as for my self in good faith my conscience so moved

me in the matter, that tho' I would not denie to sweare to the
succession, yet unto the othe that there was offered me, I
would not sweare, without the jeaparding of my soul to
perpetuall dampnacion.

It was suggested later that More's refusal to swear was due to his
following the example of Bishop Fisher of Rochester, who had also
refused to swear; but More denied this. 'I never intend to pin my
soul at another man's back, not even the best man that I know this
day living, for I knowe not whither he may happe to carry it.'
   These remarks of More have often been quoted with approval in
modern times. Since he refused to condemn other men's consciences, he appears as a forerunner of modern ideals of toleration and
respect for sincerity. In his refusal to base his conscience on anyone
else's judgement, it seems that he was foreshadowing the principle,
first clearly enunciated by Immanuel Kant, that each man must
make his own moral decisions for himself. In both these respects
More seems to contrast with the intolerance and authoritarianism
of the medieval Church and the Renaissance state.
   But if you set them back in their context, these remarks take on a
very different appearance. We discover tht the theory of conscience
which More accepted is in every respect identical with the medieval
one of Thomas Aquinas; and in many respects different from any
theory of conscience since Kant. For Aquinas, unlike Kant, the
human conscience was not a law-giver. Rather, a man's conscience
was his opinion, true or false, about the law made by God. To act
against one's conscience was always wrong, because it involved
acting against what one believed to be the law of God. But to act in
accordance with one's conscience was not always right: for one's
conscience might be an erroneous opinion. An erroneous conscience
would not excuse a man from wrongdoing, if he acted against the
clear law of God. He should have formed his conscience correctly.
And forming one's conscience was not a matter of making a
decision, or making a commitment: it was a matter of finding out a
piece of information – perhaps by consulting the scriptures, or the
councils of the Church, or it might be by reading the writings of the
saints, or by private meditation and reasoning. The only case
where a mistaken conscience would excuse from sin was when the

matter in question was a debatable one: where there was no clear scripture or council of the Church to settle the matter, and where there was a division of opinion among the saints and sacred writers.

Now, on this theory, it was obviously important that one's conscience should be properly formed. It was not enough to act in accordance with one's conscience: one's conscience must be *true*. And so More, when he told Cranmer that it would be against his conscience to swear, was careful to add: 'I have not informed my conscience either suddenly or slightly, but by long leisure and diligent search for the matter.' But for the More in Robert Bolt's play, however, what matters is not whether the Pope's supremacy is true, but the fact that More has committed his inmost self to it. As he says to Norfolk: 'What matters to me is not whether it's true or not, but that I believe it to be true, or rather not that I *believe* it, but that *I* believe it.'

The reason why More could not pin his soul to another man's back was not that he thought that each man must be his own lawgiver in morals: it was simply that no man could be trusted to persevere in correct conscience. 'There is no man living', he said, 'of whom while he liveth I may make myself sure. Some may do for favour, and some may do for fear, and so might they carry my soul a wrong way.'

Since More was convinced that he had truth on his side, how could he be sincere when he said that he condemned no man's conscience? There is a story which makes it look as if More did think a clear conscience was a sufficient passport to heaven. When his daughter, Margaret, listed all his friends who had sworn the oath, More protested that he could not swear simply for friendship's sake. 'I meddle not,' he said,

with the conscience of any man that hath sworne; nor I take not upon me to be their judge. But now, if they do well, and theyr conscience grudge them not, if I with my conscience to the contrary, should for good company pass on with them and swear as they do, when all our souls hereafter shall passe out of this world and stand in judgement at the bar before the high judge, suppose he judge them to heaven and me to the devil, because I did as they did, not thinking as they thought.

Suppose I should then say: My own good lordes and frendes, I sware because you sware, and went that way that you went, do you likewise for me now, let me not go alone, if there by any good fellowship with you, some of you come with me. I ween I should not find one that would for good fellowship go to the devil with me.

Bolt makes use of this story, but he leaves out the essential 'if' clause, 'if they do well'. More does not say here that a man will be judged to heaven simply because he acted according to his conscience: it depends whether what his conscience tells him is in fact a good thing to do. When More refused to condemn others' consciences, it was not that he did not think their judgements were incorrect. He thought so, and said so, to both Cromwell and Henry, before ever he was imprisoned in the Tower. But he did not meddle with others' consciences in the sense that he did not try to convert people to his way of thinking. Nor did he condemn them, or set himself as judge over them: 'I will not misjudge any other man's conscience', he said, 'which lyeth in their own heart far out of my sight.' But this was because the particular matters at issue – the legitimacy of the Act of Succession and the Oath thereto – were disputable matters, matters in that restricted area in which, according to the medieval theory of conscience, a man might have an erroneous conscience without moral fault.

It is quite clear that More had no *general* doctrine that conscience is a sufficient justification. This comes out from his attitude towards heretics. He never suggested that Luther and Tyndale could be excused because they were acting according to their conscience in denying Catholic doctrines. The comparison was made by Cromwell, when More refused to give a precise answer to the question whether he thought the Act of Supremacy was lawful or not. 'When you were Chancellor', Cromwell said, 'you used to compel heretics to make a precise answer whether the Pope were Head of the Church.' More replied: 'There was a difference between the two cases, because at that time, as well here as elsewhere throughout the corps of Christendom, the Pope's power was recognized for an undoubted thing which seemed not like a thing agreed in this realm, and the contrary taken for truth in other realms.' Cromwell answered: 'They were as well burned for the denying of that as they be beheaded for the denying of this; and therefore as good reason to compel them to make precise answer to the one as to the other.' And More answered: 'The reasonableness and unreasonableness in binding a man to precise answer standeth not in the respect or difference between heading and burning, but between heading and hell.'

Whenever the real More appealed against the laws of England, it was never to some private soul or self within, but to 'the whole corps of Christendom' without. And what he feared, when he refused to take the oath, was not some metaphysical spilling of his self: as he said many times, it was to suffer pain in hell, to lose the joys of heaven, and to be ungrateful to Christ who had suffered death for him.

Of course, it is no criticism of *A Man for All Seasons* to say that its hero differs from the real Thomas More. A playwright is at liberty to adapt history to his purpose. And in his preface, Robert Bolt makes it clear that he is consciously sacrificing fidelity to the historical More because most people today cannot accept More's belief in the damnation of perjurers or in a universal Church of Christ. These beliefs have to be taken as metaphors for a sense of selfhood and for society's protection against the terrifying cosmos. Bolt is surely correct in thinking that very few people today accept all More's beliefs, and some adaptation such as his is no doubt necessary to make More comprehensible.

None the less, it seems to me that the More of Bolt's play is a less consistent person than the real More. In the play it is difficult to make out what is the difference between the obstinacy with which Cromwell taunts More and the loyalty to self which More upholds. In the play it is hard to see why More should object to the heretical principles of his son-in-law, Roper. The More of the play appears to combine the most tender respect for his private conscience with an exaggerated deference to public law. Conscience and law, as the play represents them, seem to be irreconcilable values: conscience the expression of the individual will, and law the invention of the communal reason. Above all, it is hard to see why More of the play sticks where he does. Why does he both refuse to take the oath and refuse to tell anyone why he refuses? Why should his conscience make him so unbending against one of the King's laws, so anxious to comply with another?

In the More of history there was no real conflict between conscience and law: for true conscience is simply the right appreciation of God's law. A man must obey God's laws, written and unwritten; and he must in general obey man's laws provided that they do not conflict with God's laws. 'As for the law of the land,' he said,

> though every man being born and inhabiting therein is bounden to the keeping in every case upon some temporal pain and in many cases upon pain of God's displeasure too, yet is there no man bound to sweare that every law is well made nor bounden upon the pain of God's displeasure to perform any such point of the law as were in deed unlawful. Of which manner kind that there may such happen to be made in any part of Christendom I suppose no man doubteth, the general counsyl of the whole body of Christendom evermore in that point excepted.

To show that the Act of Succession was a law 'of that manner kind', More did not appeal to any metaphysical self. 'If there were no one but my self upon my side, and the whole Parlement upon the other, I wold be sore afraid,' but 'I am not bounden to change my conscience and conform it to the council of our realm, against the general council of Christendom.' Yet, so far as he could, he would obey the King's law, for fear of God's displeasure or for fear of temporal pain. For the temporal pain in question was death; and as he said to the royal commissioners: 'I have not been a man of such holy living as might be bold to offer myself to death, lest God for my presumption might suffer me to fall.'

The greatest inconsistency in *A Man for All Seasons* comes when More is condemned to death and at last feels free to speak his mind and give the reasons for his refusal to swear. Here Robert Bolt seems to have been moved more by admiration for the historical Thomas More than by desire to point his own moral. For he puts into his hero's mouth a speech almost entirely made up of verbatim quotations from the speech in Harpesfield's *Life*, which reads:

'This indictment is grounded upon an Act of Parliament directly repugnant to the laws of God and his holy Church, the supreme Government of which may no temporal Prince presume by any law to take upon him.' And then it goes on to appeal to Magna Carta and the King's Coronation Oath. In the play, this final speech has no real connection with the grounds on which More has hitherto justified his conduct. In history, it is perfectly consistent with all that went before. It was merely a public utterance of what he had all along said in private to Margaret and to the King and to Cromwell.

Rather as Bernard Shaw made Joan of Arc into a Protestant martyr, Robert Bolt has made Thomas More into an Existentialist martyr. I am sure that the real More would have enjoyed Bolt's play; but I think he would have been mightily puzzled by the conduct of its hero.

9

Descartes for Beginners

Throughout the middle ages in Europe the unquestioned scientific authority was Aristotle; for St Thomas Aquinas he was *the* philosopher; for Dante he was 'the master of those who know'. In the first half of the seventeenth century this situation was changed, for ever, by the work of the French philosopher René Descartes.

Descartes was born in 1596, at about the time when Shakespeare was writing *Hamlet*. The Reformation had divided Europe into Catholic and Protestant camps: he himself fought in the wars of religion. Though he was born and died a Catholic he spent most of his life in Protestant Holland rather than in his native country, Catholic France.

In two ways Descartes was different from the philosophers of the centuries who preceded him. He was a layman in both the ecclesiastical and the professional sense. Whereas all the great philosophers of the middle ages had been churchmen – priests, bishops, friars – Descartes was a man of the world, a gentleman of leisure living on his fortune. And while all the medieval philosophers had been university professors teaching courses in a technical language, Descartes never gave a lecture in his life, and often wrote for the general reader. His most famous work, the *Discourse on Method*, was written not in the Latin of the learned world, but in good plain French, so that it could be understood, as he put it, 'even by women'.

Descartes was a man of quite extraordinary genius. Nowadays it is his philosophical works which are most read: in his own time his reputation rested as much on his mathematical and scientific works. He was the founder of analytical geometry, and the Cartesian coordinates that every schoolchild learns about derive their name from the Latin form of his name, Cartesius. In his thirties he wrote a treatise on dioptrics which was a substantial contribution to the science of optics, the result of careful theoretical and experimental work on the nature of the eye and of light. He also composed one of the first scientific treatises on meteorology, and has a claim to be the first man to discover the true nature of rainbows.

The culmination of his early scientific work was a treatise called *The World*. In it he set out to give an exhaustive scientific account of the origin and nature of the universe, and of the working of the human body. In it he adopted the then unusual hypothesis, that the sun, and not the earth, is the centre of our universe. As he was completing his work he learnt that the astronomer Galileo had been condemned by the church authorities in Italy for defending the same heliocentric system. This made him decide not to publish his treatise: he kept it in his files until his death. By the time he was forty, he had acquired a reputation among a circle of friends as something of a genius but he had still not published a word.

In 1637 he decided to publish his dioptrics, his geometry and his meteorology; and he prefaced these works with a brief *Discourse on Method*. The three scientific treatises are now read only by specialists in the history of science; but the preface is reprinted every year, has been translated into more than a hundred languages, and is still read with pleasure by millions who could not understand the works to which it was an introduction.

In the first place, it is a delicious piece of autobiographical writing: vivid, urbane, ironic. A few extracts will give its flavour.

> . . . as soon as my age allowed me to pass from under the control of my instructors, I entirely abandoned the study of letters, and resolved not to seek after any science but what might be found within myself or in the great book of the world. So I spent the rest of my youth in travel, in frequenting courts and armies, in mixing with people of various dispositions and ranks and in collecting a variety of experiences.

. . . from college days I had learnt that one can imagine
nothing so strange and incredible but has been said by some
philosopher; and since then, while travelling, I have realised
that those whose opinions are quite opposed to ours are not,
for all that, without exception barbarians and savages; many
of them enjoy as good a share of reason as we do, or better.

. . . it is by custom and example that we are persuaded, much
more than by any certain knowledge; at the same time, a
majority of votes is worthless as a proof, in regard to truths
that are even a little difficult of discovery; for it is much more
likely that one man should have hit upon them for himself
than that a whole nation should. Accordingly I could choose
nobody whose opinions I thought preferable to other men's;
and I was as it were forced to become my own guide.[1]

The *Discourse* presents, in an astonishingly small compass, a
summary of Descartes's scientific views and of his philosophic
method. He could present complicated philosophical doctrines so
elegantly that they appeared fully intelligible on first reading and
yet still provide matter for reflection to the most advanced
specialists. He prided himself that his works could be read 'just like
novels'. Indeed, his main ideas can be so concisely expressed that
they could be written on the back of a postcard; and yet they were
so revolutionary that they changed the course of philosophy for
centuries.

If you wanted to put Descartes' main ideas on the back of a
postcard you would need just two sentences: man is a thinking
mind; matter is extension in motion. Everything, in Descartes's
system, is to be explained in terms of this dualism of mind and
matter. Indeed, we owe to Descartes that we think of mind and
matter as the two great, mutually exclusive and mutually exhaustive, divisions of the universe we inhabit.

For Descartes, man is a thinking substance. In the philosophy of
Aristotle man is essentially a composite of soul and body;
disembodied existence, if possible at all, is a maimed and

---

[1] Descartes, *Philosophical Writings*, ed. Anscombe and Geach (London, Nelson 1966),
pp. 12–13, 18–19.

incomplete human existence. For Descartes, man's whole essence is mind: in the present life our minds are intimately united with our bodies, but it is not our bodies that make us what we really are. Moreover mind is conceived in a new way: the essence of mind is not intelligence but consciousness, awareness of one's own thoughts and their objects. Man is the *only* conscious animal; all other animals, Descartes believed, are merely complicated, but unconscious, machines.

For Descartes, matter is extension in motion. By 'extension' is meant what has the geometrical properties of shape, size, divisibility and so on; these were the *only* properties which Descartes attributed, at a fundamental level, to matter. He offered to explain all of the phenomena of heat, light, colour and sound in terms of the motion of small particles of different sizes and shapes. Descartes is one of the first systematic exponents of the idea of modern Western science as a combination of mathematical procedures and experimental methods.

Both of the great principles of Cartesian philosophy were – we now know – false. In his own lifetime phenomena were discovered which were incapable of straightforward explanation in terms of matter in motion. The circulation of the blood and of the action of the heart, as discovered by the English John Harvey, demanded the operation of forces for which there was no room in Descartes's system. None the less, his scientific account of the origin and nature of the world was fashionable for a century or so after his death; and his conception of animals as machines was later extended by some of his disciples who claimed, to the shocked horror of their contemporaries, that human beings too were only complicated machines.

Descartes's view of the nature of mind endured much longer than his view of matter: indeed, it is still the most widespread view of mind among educated people in the West who are not professional philosophers. In our own century it has been decisively refuted by the work of the Austrian philosopher, Ludwig Wittgenstein, who showed that even when we think our most private and spiritual thoughts we are employing the medium of a language which is essentially tied to its public and bodily expression. We now know, thanks to Wittgenstein, that the Cartesian dichotomy of mind and body is untenable. But it is a measure of the enormous influence of Descartes that even those who most admire the genius of Wittgenstein think that his greatest achievement was the overthrow of Descartes's philosophy of mind.

Descartes said that knowledge was like a tree, whose roots were metaphysics, whose trunk was physics, and whose fruitful branches were the moral and useful sciences. His own writings, after the *Discourse*, followed the order thus suggested. In 1641 he wrote his metaphysical *Meditations*, in 1644 his *Principles of Philosophy* (an edited version of *The World*) in the 1649 a *Treatise on the Passions* which is largely an ethical treatise. The 1640s were the final, most philosophically fruitful, decade of his life.

One way in which Descartes profoundly influenced later philosophy was to insist that the first task of the philosopher is to rid himself of all prejudice by calling in doubt all that can be doubted. This puts epistemology, or the methodical study of what we can know, in the first place in philosophy. The second task of the philosopher, having raised these doubts, is to prevent them leading to scepticism. This comes out clearly in Descartes's *Meditations*. Here are some extracts from the first Meditation in which the sceptical doubts are raised.

What I have so far accepted as true *par excellence*, I have got either from the senses or by means of the senses. Now I have sometimes caught the senses deceiving me; and a wise man never entirely trusts those who have once cheated him.

But although the senses may sometimes deceive us about some minute or remote objects, yet there are many other facts as to which doubt is plainly impossible, although these are gathered from the same source: e.g. that I am here, sitting by the fire, wearing a winter cloak, holding this paper in my hands, and so on.

A fine argument! As though I were not a man who habitually sleeps at night and has the same impressions (or even wilder ones) in sleep as these men do when awake! How often, in the still of the night, I have the familiar conviction that I am here, wearing a cloak, sitting by the fire – when really I am undressed and lying in bed!

Well, suppose I am dreaming . . . Whether I am awake or asleep, two and three add up to five, and a square has only four sides; and it seems impossible for such obvious truths to fall under a suspicion of being false.

But there has been implanted in my mind the old opinion that there is a God who can do everything, and who made me such as I am. How do I know he has not brought it about that, while in fact there is no earth, no sky, no extended objects, no shape, no size, no place, yet all these things should appear to exist as they do now? Moreover, I judge that other men sometimes go wrong over what they think they know perfectly well; may not God likewise make me go wrong, whenever I add two and three, or count the sides of a square, or do any simpler thing that might be imagined? But perhaps it was not God's will to deceive me so; he is after all called supremely good.

I will suppose, then, not that there is a supremely good God, the source of truth; but that there is an evil spirit, who is supremely powerful and intelligent, and does his utmost to deceive me. I will suppose that sky, air, earth, colours, shapes, sounds and all external objects are mere delusive dreams, by means of which he lays snares for my credulity. I will consider myself as having no hands, no eyes, no flesh, no blood, no senses, but just having a false belief that I have all these things. I will remain firmly fixed in this meditation, and resolutely take care that, so far as in me lies, even if it is not in my power to know some truth, I may not assent to falsehood nor let myself be imposed upon by that deceiver, however powerful and intelligent he may be.

These doubts are brought to an end by Descartes's famous argument to his own existence. However much the evil genius may deceive him, it can never deceive him into thinking that he exists when he does not. 'I think, therefore I exist', says Descartes and then he proceeds in the rest of the Meditation to answer the question, '*What* am I, this I whom I know to exist?'

Descartes's publications brought him fame throughout Europe. He entered into correspondence and controversy with most of the learned men of his time. Some of his friends began to read his views in universities: and the *Principles of Philosophy* was designed as a textbook. Other professors, seeing their Aristotelian system threatened, subjected the new doctrines to violent attack. Even in the comparatively tolerant environment of Holland, Descartes felt the blast of religious persecution.

However, he did not lack powerful friends and was therefore never in serious danger. Princess Elizabeth of the Palatine, a niece of King Charles I of England, was enchanted by his works and wrote him many letters. She was quite capable of holding her own in argument, and out of their correspondence grew the last of Descartes's full-length works, the *Passions of the Soul*. When it was published, however, it was dedicated not to Elizabeth but to another royal lady who had interested herself in philosophy, Queen Christina of Sweden. Against his better judgement Descartes was persuaded to accept appointment as court philosopher to Queen Christina, who sent an admiral with a battleship to fetch him from Holland to Stockholm.

Descartes had immense confidence in his own abilities and still more in the method which he had discovered. He thought given a few more years of life, and given sufficient funds for his experiments, he would be able to solve all the outstanding problems of physiology, and learn thereby the cures of all diseases. Perhaps he never knew how chimerical was this hope: for his life was cut short by his ill-advised acceptance of a position at the Swedish court. Queen Christina insisted on being given her philosophy lessons at 5 o'clock in the morning; under this regime Descartes soon fell a victim to the rigours of a Swedish winter and died in 1650 of one of the diseases whose cure he had vainly hoped was within the grasp of his methods. There was a strange and ironic fittingness about the epitaph which he had chosen as his own motto.

> No man is harmed by death, save he
> who, known too well by all the world,
> has not yet learnt to know himself.

> Illi mors gravis incubat
> Qui, notus nimis omnibus
> Ignotus moritur sibi.

10

Descartes's Ontological Argument

I

In the *Discourse on Method*, Descartes says:

> I saw quite well that, assuming a triangle, its three angles
> must be equal to two right angles; but for all that I saw
> nothing that assured me that there was any triangle in the real
> world. On the other hand, going back to an examination of my
> idea of a perfect Being, I found that this included the existence
> of such a Being; in the same way as the idea of a triangle
> includes the equality of its three angles to two right angles, or
> the idea of a sphere includes the equidistance of all parts [of its
> surface] from the centre; or indeed, in an even more evident
> way. Consequently it is at least as certain that God, the
> perfect Being in question, is or exists, as any proof in geometry
> can be (IV).

Let us take the steps of this proof in turn. What is meant by
'assuming a triangle' (*supposant une triangle*)? Does it mean:
assuming some triangle exists? Gilson glosses: 'the supposition that
a triangle be given, whether it exist really or not' and appeals to the
Latin text: *si exempli causa supponamus dari aliquod triangulum*. But so
far as this text goes, we seem to have two alternatives: (1) If a
triangle exists, it has its three angles equal to two right angles.
(2) Any triangle, whether it exists or not, has its three angles equal
to two right angles.

We may notice that neither of these formulations can be translated into Frege–Russell notation; and we may notice, too, as Descartes says, that neither contains any assurance 'that there is any triangle in the real world'.

Further light is thrown on Descartes's meaning by a passage in the Fifth Meditation. 'When I imagine a triangle, it may be that no such figure exists anywhere outside my thought, or never has existed; but there certainly is its determinate nature, its essence, its form (*est tamen profecto determinata quaedam eius natura, sive essentia, sive forma*), which is unchangeable and eternal. This is no figment of mine, and does not depend on my mind, as is clear from the following: various properties can be proved of this triangle, e.g. that its three angles are together equal to two right angles, that its greatest side subtends its greatest angle, and so on' (AT VII, 64).[1] He says (a little above) that this is an example of 'things which, even if they perhaps exist nowhere outside me, cannot be said to be nothing'.

This passage, by substituting for the phrase 'to be in the world' of the *Discourse* the phrase 'exist outside my thought', brings in by implicit contrast the notion of 'existence in thought'. Moreover, unlike the *Discourse* passage, it distinguishes between the triangle, on the one hand, and the nature or essence or form of the triangle on the other. Further, it adds a more fortunate example of an eternal and immutable property of a triangle than the one Descartes uses in setting forth the ontological argument. Since the development of non-Euclidean geometries it is no longer true to say that the three angles of a triangle must equal two rights angles. Some would say this reveals, at this point, a fundamental misconception of Descartes concerning the nature of geometry; to me it seems to show simply that he chose a poor example of what he had in mind. His second example is better: even of non-Euclidean triangles it is true that the greatest side subtends the greatest angle. It would be possible, I think, to safeguard Descartes from criticism on this point by substituting this example for the other one wherever it occurs in his statement of his proof. However, I will not do so, but will proceed as if it were a geometrical truth that the three angles of any triangle equal two right angles.

[1] AT = Charles Adam and Paul Tannery, *Oeuvres de Descartes*, (Paris, 1897, 1913).

It is clear, I think, that what Descartes means by a triangle existing in the world, or existing outside thought, is for there to be in the world some body which has a triangular shape. Clearly, someone who is in doubt whether any body exists at all does not know whether, in this sense, any triangle exists in the world. But the supposition that no triangles exist in the world is not merely a part of Descartes's hyperbolical doubt. He believed the supposition to be true of the macroscopic world even after he had provided the solution to his methodic doubts. 'I do not agree that these [geometric figures] have ever fallen under our senses, as everyone normally believes, because though there is no doubt that there could be in the world figures such as the geometers consider, I deny that there are any around us, unless perhaps they be so small that they make no impression on our senses; because they are for the most part made up of straight lines, and I not think that any part of a line has touched our senses which was strictly straight' – and he appeals to the way straight lines look wavy under a magnifying glass (AT VII, 381).

These passages, it seems to me, make it likely that it is (2), and not (1), which Descartes has in mind. The theorem about the angles of a triangle is not meant to be a counterfactual about what would be the case if there were, as there are not, triangles existent in the world. It is meant to be an actual statement about something which can be a subject of predication even when there are no triangles in existence. But the question arises: in the absence of existent triangles, *what* is it that has the properties ascribed by the theorems?

Hobbes raised this question in his fourteenth objection. 'If a triangle exists nowhere, I do not understand how it can have a nature; for what is nowhere, is not, and therefore has not a being or a nature. . . . The truth of the proposition "a triangle is something having its three angles equal to two right angles" is everlasting. But the nature of a triangle is not everlasting; all triangles might cease to be.' Similarly, the proposition 'Man is an animal' is true for ever, because names are everlasting, but when the human race ceases to be, human nature will be no more. Hobbes's objection is wrapped up in his theory that to predicate is to attach a second name to something; but it is independent of that theory. Descartes replied:

'Everybody is familiar with the distinction of essence and existence; and this talk about names as being everlasting (instead of our having notions or ideas of eternal truths) has already been sufficiently refuted.'

This reply is hardly adequate. But the following reply seems open to Descartes. What exists nowhere, neither in the world nor in thought, can have no nature, perhaps; but the triangle exists in thought, and has a true and immutable nature which persists whether or not any triangles outside thought exist or cease to be.

Let us explore that possible reply. Notice first that what has the properties which the theorems prove is not, strictly, the essence or nature of the triangle; the essence and properties belong to something, and the essence is made up of the properties which the theorems prove. But to *what* do these properties belong? What *has* the nature of a triangle whether or not any triangle exists? The text of the *Meditations* is ambiguous. '*Invenio apud me innumeras ideas quarumdam rerum, quae, etiam si extra me fortasse nullibi existant, non tamen dici possunt nihil esse; & quamvis a me quoddamodo ad arbitrium cogitentur, non tamen a me finguntur, sed suas habent veras et immutabiles naturas*' (AT VIII, 64). Is it the *ideae* or the *res* which has their true and immutable natures? Neither the Latin nor the French text settles it.[2] He goes on to speak of the properties which can be proved *de isto triangulo*, which seems to suggest that that to which the properties belong is a triangle. But there seems something very odd about a triangle which exists whether or not any triangle exists; and *iste triangulus* is the triangle which I imagine, so that the phrase may mean, not a triangle, but the idea of a triangle. On the other hand, we might say that the triangle of which the properties are proved is indeed a triangle but not one which exists, merely one which *datur*, which is given; *being given* to be understood as something between existence and nothingness: for it is certainly of *res*, and not of ideas, that Descartes says 'non tamen dici possunt nihil esse'. This seems a slightly more natural way of reading the text, and accords with the *Discourse on Method* which does not mention ideas. But if we read it thus, further difficulties arise.

---

[2] For *ideae: ad arbitrium cogitentur*: thought at will; it is ideas which are thought. For *res*: the *quae* before the colon refers to *res*; *cogitentur* would be thought *of*; natures more naturally belong to *res*. The gender is the same in both Latin and French.

What is the relation between the *dari* of the triangle and the occurrence of the idea of the triangle? Can we say that for the triangle, *dari est cogitari*? Or is it possible for a triangle to be given without being thought of? If it is a triangle which has an eternal and immutable nature, then it seems that *dari* cannot be identified with *cogitari*. For Descartes says 'it is not necessary for me ever to imagine any triangle; but whenever I choose to consider a rectilinear figure that has just three angles, I must ascribe to it properties from which it is rightly inferred that its three angles are not greater than two right angles' (AT VII, 67). Now Descartes has just said – a propos of the idea of God – that his thought imposes no necessity on things, but the necessity of the thing determines him to think (ibid., lines 5 ff.). Analogously, he should say that this necessity of ascribing certain properties to a triangle whenever he thinks of it comes from the triangle, not from his thought. Again, we reach the conclusion that what has the eternal and immutable nature is a triangle, not the idea of a triangle; and we add to this conclusion that this triangle, which has the provable properties, *datur*, whether or not Descartes or anyone ever has an idea of a triangle. This means that we must modify what we imagined Descartes as replying to Hobbes: when Hobbes says that only what exists can have a nature, Descartes must reply that not only what exists in the world, and not only what exists in the mind, but also that which is given, whether or not it exists, has a nature.

I do not think we need to make any further distinction between the givenness of the triangle and the being of the nature of the triangle. When Descartes says '*est profecto determinata quaedam eius natura*' (AT VII, 64, 15) I take the '*eius*' to mean 'of the triangle'; and I take it that '*est natura determinata trianguli*' means the same as '*datur triangulus determinatam habens naturam*'; the two differ, I take it, merely in being abstract and concrete ways of saying the same thing.

If I am right, we have in Descartes's apparatus three possible different states of affairs:

> triangulus datur
> triangulus cogitatur
> triangulus existit

That to which '*triangulus*' refers in each of these cases is the same, though only in the second case is there an idea of a triangle, and only in the third case is there an actually existent triangle.

Let us see if we can confirm this reading from the presentations of the ontological argument elsewhere, and from the answers to the objections. In the definitions which open the geometric proof of the existence of God in the *Second Replies*, we read: 'When we say that some attribute is contained in the nature or the concept of a thing, it is the same as if we were to say that this attribute is true of that thing' (AT VII, 162). The thing referred to here must be something distinct from an *existent* thing; otherwise the ontological argument based on this definition is a blatant *petitio principii*; and indeed it would be possible, by the ontological argument, to prove the existence of something corresponding to every conceivable nature.

In the *Principles* we read that when mind contemplates its idea without affirming or denying that there is anything outside itself which corresponds to these ideas, it is beyond any danger of falling into error. As an example of the demonstrations which are possible within this field, we are given: that the three angles of a triangle are equal to two right angles. The mind, we are told, because it sees that it is necessarily involved in the idea of the triangle that it should have three angles which are equal to two right angles, is absolutely persuaded that the triangle has three angles equal to two right angles. Now the triangle which is here spoken of is not an existent triangle; for the mind is supposed to be taking care neither to affirm nor deny that anything outside itself corresponds to its ideas. Nor, it seems, is it the idea of the triangle; for the statement that the triangle has three angles equal to two right angles is presented not as a statement about the idea of the triangle, but as a conclusion which is drawn from reflection on the idea of the triangle. And this is borne out by the parallel deduction of the existence of a perfect Being (AT VIII, 9–10).

Perhaps the fullest working out of the ontological argument comes in the *First Answers* (AT VIII, 115 ff.). The kernel of the argument is stated thus: That which we clearly and distinctly understand to belong to the true and immutable nature of anything, its essence or form, can be truly affirmed of that thing. This again cannot be the existent thing, for that would involve a gross begging of the question when applied to the nature of God. This major premise is not argued for by Descartes in this place, because he says it has already been agreed by the objector that whatever we clearly and distinctly perceive is true (HR II, 19).[3] Now strictly, there is a leap here: from this principle, plus the fact that we clearly and distinctly understand some property to belong to the true and immutable nature of something, it follows only that the property in question does belong to the true and immutable nature of the thing, not that it can be truly affirmed of it. But provided we take the thing to which the property belongs to be a not necessarily existent thing, then the leap is not a big one: it involves only the further principle that what has a nature has the properties which belong to the nature. But if we take it that properties can only be affirmed of existent things, the leap is fallacious; for something might belong to the nature of triangle, and yet not be true of any triangle, because no triangle existed.

A little further on Descartes says, 'If I think of a triangle . . . then I shall truly affirm of the triangle all the things which I recognize to be contained in the idea of the triangle, as that its angles are equal to two right angles, etc.' Once again, the triangle of which this property is truly affirmed is not any existent triangle. But what is the relation between the *nature* of the not-necessarily-existent triangle, and the *idea* of a triangle? It is not that every time I think of a triangle, I think of everything which is contained in the nature of the triangle. 'Though I can think of a triangle while restricting my thought in such a manner that I do not think at all of its three angles being equal to two right angles, yet I cannot deny that attribute of it by any clear and distinct mental operation, i.e. rightly understanding what I say.' So whatever belongs to the nature of a triangle is contained in the idea of a triangle; but not every time that I think of a triangle do I think of what is contained in the idea of a triangle (AT VII, 117; HR II, 20).

It seems to be true in general that whatever belongs to the nature of X is contained in the idea of X; but the converse is not true, that wherever we have an idea containing certain elements there is some nature composed of corresponding elements. The idea of a triangle

[3] HR = Elizabeth Haldane and G Ross, *The Philosophical Works of Descartes* (Cambridge, 1907, 1911).

is both simple and innate; others are composite and factitious. Some composite ideas have natures corresponding to them. Take, for instance, the idea of a triangle inscribed in a square. It is not part of the nature of a triangle to be so inscribed, nor part of the nature of a square to contain such a triangle. None the less, the composite figure itself has a true and immutable nature, and accordingly, certain properties are true of it, e.g. that the area of the square cannot be less than double that of the inscribed triangle. But others do not. The idea, for instance, of a Hippogriff or winged horse is a composite and factitious idea (AT VII, 37). This comes out in the control which the mind has over such ideas. 'Those ideas which do not contain a true and immutable nature, but only a fictitious one put together by the mind, can be divided by the same mind, not merely by abstraction or restriction of thought but by a clear and distinct operation.' What mind has put together, mind can put asunder. 'For example, when I think of a winged horse . . . I easily understand that I can on the contrary think of a horse without wings' – not just think of a horse without thinking of his wings, but think of a horse without wings, clearly understanding what I'm talking about. So here we have an idea which contains the property of being winged, plus the properties constituting the nature of horse; but there is no thing, existent or non-existent, which has these properties as its nature (AT VII, 117).

I do not think that Descartes makes clear what is supposed to be the difference between the winged horse and the triangle inscribed in the square. If I can think of a horse without wings, equally I can think of a triangle not inscribed in a square. If I cannot think of a triangle-in-a-square without certain properties, equally I cannot think of a winged horse without wings. Perhaps the difference is this: The properties of a winged horse are just the sum total of the properties of a horse and the properties of being winged. But the proportion which Descartes mentions as a property of a triangle inscribed in a square is not a property of a triangle as such, considered without reference to any square; nor is it a property of a square as such, considered without reference to any triangle. 'I cannot think of a winged horse without wings' is true because I cannot think of a winged X without wings, no matter what X may be. 'I cannot think of a triangle inscribed in an X which is more than half the area of the figure in which it is inscribed' is not true no matter what X may be.

Descartes's views as I have expounded them bear a strong resemblance to those of Meinong. Just as Descartes distinguishes between '*datur*' and '*existere*', so Meinong makes a distinction between '*es gibt*' and '*sein*'. For Descartes not only what exists has a nature but also what is given has a nature. Similarly, Meinong writes, 'The figures with which geometry is concerned do not exist. Nevertheless their properties can be established.' He called this the principle of the independence of *Sosein* from *Sein*. For Descartes it is not necessary that there should be an idea of X for a non-existent X to be given and have properties. Similarly, Meinong wrote, 'it is no more necessary to an object that it be presented [to the mind] in order not to exist than it is in order for it to exist.' For Descartes there is something which is a triangle whether or not any triangle exists. Such a triangle is surely very like a Meinongian Pure Object, which 'stands beyond being and non-being'.[4]

Within the realm of being, Meinong makes a further distinction between subsistence (*Bestand*) and existence (*Existenz*). He gives as examples of things which subsist: similarities, differences, numbers, logical connections, or the existence of the antipodes. If two objects are similar, then there subsists a similarity between them. Roughly, subsistence appears to be the being of abstract objects, and existence appears to be the being of concrete objects. The corresponding distinction in Descartes would seem to be that between two sorts of being or *entitas*, namely modal being (*entitas modalis*) which belongs to the attributes of things, and reality (*realitas*) which belongs only to substances. 'Whatever is real can exist separately from any other subject; and whatever can exist thus separately is a substance' (VII, 434; cf. AT III, 430; VII, 253, 364).

II

So far we have been considering the first stage of Descartes's ontological argument, his statement that 'assuming a triangle, its

---

[4] See Meinong's Theory of Objects, translated in Roderick M. Chisholm (ed.), *Realism and the Background of Phenomenology* (Glencoe, 1960), pp. 76 ff. The passages quoted are from pp. 82, 83, 86 respectively.

three angles must be equal to two right angles'. We must now turn
to his application of his principles. 'Going back to an examination
of my idea of a perfect Being, I found that this included the
existence of such a being. Consequently . . . it is . . . certain that
God, the perfect being in question, is or exists.' So the *Discourse*,
arguing from the idea of God. The *Meditations* reaches the same
conclusion from a consideration of the essence of God. 'I clearly see
that existence can no more be separated from the essence of God
than can its having three angles equal to two right angles be
separated from the essence of a triangle, or the idea of a mountain
from the idea of a valley; and so there is no less absurdity in
thinking of a God (a supremely perfect being) who lacks existence
than in thinking of a mountain without a valley' (AT VII, 66).

Gassendi, anticipating Kant, objected that existence should not
be compared in this manner with a property. 'Neither in God nor in
anything else is existence a perfection, but rather that without
which there are no perfections . . . Existence can't be said to exist
in a thing like a perfection; and if a thing lacks existence, then it is
not just imperfect or lacking perfection; it is nothing at all. When
you were listing the perfections of a triangle, you did not count
existence, and you did not draw any conclusion about the existence
of the triangle. Similarly, when listing the perfections of God, you
should not have included existence, or drawn the conclusion that
God exists, unless you want to beg the question' (AT VII, 323).

Descartes replied: 'I do not see what sort of thing you want
existence to be, nor why it can't be called a property just as much
as omnipotence, provided that we use the word "property" for any
attribute, or whatever can be predicated of a thing' (VII, 382).
Fairly clearly, he had missed the point of Gassendi's criticism, but
equally, Gassendi's remarks were based in their turn on a
misunderstanding. He did not realize that for Descartes, the
subject of the sentence 'God exists' was a pure object, beyond being
and non-being. A pure object can have properties whether or not it
exists; but if we are inquiring about its properties, one of the most
interesting questions we can ask is 'does it exist or not?' In making
predications of a pure object we are not begging the question of its
existence; and when Descartes concludes 'God exists' from the
premise 'God is supremely perfect' he is drawing his conclusion not

from the occurrence of the word 'God' in the subject-place of his premise, but because he believes the predicate 'exists' is included in the predicate 'is supremely perfect'. The objection 'existence is not a predicate' amounts to this: 'exists' cannot be a predicate because if it is false of any subject then there is no such subject for it to be false of. But this objection has no force unless there is an independent argument to show that Meinongian pure objects are incoherent. For even if there is no God, so that 'God exists' is false, there is always the appropriate pure object to sustain the false predicate.

Hume denied that existence could form part of the content of an idea. 'The idea of existence is nothing different from the idea of any object, and when after the simple conception of any thing we would conceive it as existent, we in reality make no addition or alteration on our first idea' (*Treatise*, I, III, 7). The idea of an existent X is the same as the idea of an X. Descartes to some extent anticipated this line of objection. 'We never think of things without thinking of them as existents' he wrote (AT VIII, 117). All ideas, therefore, in a sense contain existence (AT VII, 166). But whereas the ideas of other things contain possible existence, the idea of God contains necessary existence. The mind sees that in the idea of a supremely perfect being, 'there is contained existence – not merely possible and contingent existence, as in the ideas of all other things which it distinctly perceives, but altogether necessary and eternal existence' (AT VII, 116, VIII, 10).

Descartes's meaning seems to be this. Take the defining properties of any entity; let 'F' represent a predicate-term for those properties. If we can clearly and distinctly conceive of an entity which is F, then we know that it is *possible* for an entity which is F to exist. In the case of God, however, we can draw a stronger conclusion. Where the properties in question are those which define God, we know that it is *necessary* for an entity which is F to exist. 'We conceive clearly that actual existence is necessarily and always conjoint with the other attributes of God' (AT, VII, 116).

This is proved by Descartes in two distinct manners. Commonly, he argues that since God is perfect, and existence is a perfection, it follows necessarily that God exists (AT VII, 66; 166; also *Discourse on Method*). In the *First Replies*, it is not from God's perfection but from His omnipotence that the argument is drawn. 'Because we cannot think of God's existence as being possible, without at the same time, and by taking heed of His immeasurable power, acknowledging that He can exist by His own might, we hence conclude that He really exists and has existed from all eternity; for the light of nature makes it most plain that what can exist by its own power always exists' (AT VII, 119).

This last passage creates a peculiar mental discomfort; at least, we feel, there must be some important premises suppressed. Descartes himself was not altogether happy about the argument. At first he had written thus: 'We cannot think of His existence as being possible without at the same time thinking that it must be possible for there to be some power by means of which He exists; and that power cannot be conceived to be in anything else than in that same supremely powerful being; and so we conclude that He can exist by His own might.' But before these words went to the printer, he asked Mersenne to cancel them so that the curious could not decipher them, in case anybody attacked the author 'in the place which he himself judged to be the weakest' (AT III, 330).

The stages of the argument seem to be as follows:

(1) God's existence is possible. This is shown because we have a clear and distinct idea of God (AT VII, 119); and this in turn is proved because 'whatever I clearly and distinctly perceive, which is real and true and involves some perfection is all contained in [the idea of God]' (AT VII, 46) (cf. VII, 150). This is the part of the argument which Leibniz thought deficient. It needed to be proved, he said, that all perfections were compatible with each other; otherwise the idea of an all-perfect being would imply a contradiction. Leibniz himself was prepared to offer such a proof, which convinced Spinoza but has not satisfied modern critics.[5]

(2) God is by definition all-powerful and independent. This is said in the third Meditation (VII, 45, etc.). It followed from this, Descartes thought, that if He can exist at all He can exist by his own power. But we know that God can exist. Therefore:

(3) God can exist by his own power.

---

[5] It is, however, accepted by Russell: *Philosophy of Leibniz*, (London, Allen & Unwin, 1900), p. 174.

(4) What can exist by its own power, does exist. It is this step which at first sight seems most in need of justification. I suggest that there are two suppressed premisses. (a) If you can do something by your own power, and you do not do it, then it can only be because you do not want to do it; (b) everything wants to exist. Now (a) is plausible enough, and is commonly accepted when it is appealed to in a famous formulation of the Problem of Evil ('If God can prevent evils, and does not prevent them, then he must not want to prevent them'); (b) sounds odd to us, but in fact *omnia appetunt esse* was a scholastic commonplace. Now (a) and (b) together yield (4), and (3) and (4) together give:

(5) God exists.

One misgiving which we may feel here concerns the application of (b) to Pure Objects. We may be prepared to go so far with Descartes and Meinong as to admit that non-existent entities can have natures and properties, but surely they cannot have *desires*? This misgiving sems unfounded. If we are to make predications of the non-existent at all, among the predications we must make will be some which involve desires. For instance, we shall have to say that centaurs (though no centaurs exist) have the libidinous appetites ascribed to them by classical authorities. A non-libidinous centaur would not be a centaur at all.

The premisses from which Descartes here derives the existence of God have always been true; therefore he concludes not only that God exists, but that he has existed from all eternity. 'For the light of nature makes it most plain that what can exist by its own power always exists.'

The light of nature can do so, I contend, only if it shows us also that everything desires existence. '*Omnia appetunt esse*' is explicitly supplied by Aquinas as a suppressed premise to rescue from fallacy an argument of Aristotle's which purported to show that whatever can corrupt sometimes does corrupt, so that any everlasting being must be a necessary being.[6] Now when scholastics spoke of 'necessary being' they did not mean a being whose existence was a necessary truth; they meant a being which, in the order of nature, could not cease to exist. For medieval Aristotelians the stars were

---

[6] Cf. C. J. F. Williams, Aristotle and Corruptability, *Religious Studies*, 1, 19, who quotes Aquinas *in lib*. I *de Caelo et Mundo, lectio* xxvi, n. 6.

necessary beings in this sense. Their existence was not a necessary truth; it was contingent on the will of God, who might never have created. But they were naturally indestructible, and could cease to exist only by being annihilated by their creator. Obviously, something whose existence was a logically necessary truth, would *a fortiori* be necessary in the scholastic sense; but the converse does not hold.

It is important to underline this distinction. A recent revival of the Ontological Argument runs as follows: 'If God, a being greater that which cannot be conceived, does not exist, then He cannot come into existence . . . Since He cannot come into existence, if He does not exist His existence is impossible. If He does exist, He cannot have come into existence . . . nor can He cease to exist, for nothing could cause Him to cease to exist nor could it just happen that He ceased to exist. So if God exists, His existence is necessary. Thus God's existence is either impossible or necessary. It can be the former only if the concept of such a being is self-contradictory or in some way logically absurd. Assuming that this is not so, it follows that He necessarily exists.'[7]

In this argument there is a fallacy: 'impossible' is being used in two senses, in one of which it is contrasted with the modern notion of logical necessity, in the other of which it is contrasted with the medieval notion of necessary being. In the first sense it means 'involving the violation of a logical truth', in the second it means 'incapable of being brought into or put out of existence'. The statement 'If God does not exist His existence is impossible' may be true in the sense that if God does not exist he cannot be brought into existence, without being true in the sense, that if God does not exist, the statement 'God exists' must involve the violation of a logical truth. But it must be true in the latter sense if the argument is to work.

Now it might seem that an analogous fallacy is being committed by Descartes when he argues that if God can exist at all, He can exist by his own power. For does not the first 'can' refer to logical possibility, whereas the second 'can' relates to powers residing in natural agents? I think, in fact, Descartes's argument does not

---

[7] N. Malcolm, 'Anselm's Ontological Argument', *Philosophical Review*, *49 (1960) p. 48.*

contain this fallacy, though it moves rather too fast. Premise (1) above certainly only shows that it is logically possible for God to exist, not that God has any power to exist. That God has the power to exist follows not from premise (1), but from the different premise that God is all-powerful: he can do everything, including exist. That God can exist *by his own power* follows from this plus the premise that God is independent, i.e. that he can do whatever he can do without help from anything else. That this is the line of Descartes's thought is I think shown by the passage which he ordered Mersenne to cancel, though we may well sympathize with his despairing of presenting it in a clear and plausible manner.

Certainly, Descartes was aware of the possibility of the fallacious argument recorded above, and he pointed out the fallacy. In the *Second Replies* he discusses the argument, 'If it is not self-contradictory for God to exist, then it is certain that he exists; but it is not self-contradictory for him to exist; *ergo* . . . ' This argument, he says, is a sophism. 'For in the major the word "self-contradictory" has reference to the concept of a cause from which God would derive existence; in the minor, however, it refers only to the concept of the divine existence and nature. This is clear from the following. If the major is denied, it is proved as follows: if God does not yet exist, it is self-contradictory for him to exist, because there cannot be any cause sufficient to produce Him; but it is not self-contradictory for him to exist, *ergo* . . . But if the minor is denied, we shall have to say that is not self-contradictory, in the formal concept of which there is nothing which involves a contradition; but in the formal concept of the divine existence or nature there is nothing which involves a contradiction, *ergo* . . . And these two are very different.' Descartes's God exists necessarily, in the sense that 'God exists' is a necessary truth.

It seems to me that if we give Descartes his Meinongian assumptions, there is nothing fallacious in his argument. This makes it the more extraordinary that Meinong himself did not accept the ontological argument. When he said that objects as such were beyond being and not being, Meinong was careful to add qualifications. 'This is not to say, of course, that an Object can neither be nor not be. Nor is it to say that the question, whether or not the Object has being, is purely accidental to the nature of every

Object. An absurd Object such as a round square carries in itself the guarantee of its own non-being in every sense; an ideal Object, such as diversity, carries in itself the guarantee of its own non-existence.' If this is so, one might ask Meinong, why cannot there be an Object which carries in itself the guarantee of its own existence?

Russell, reviewing Meinong in *Mind* 1905 (p. 533) claimed that he could not in consistency reject the ontological proof.

> If the round square is round and square the existent round square is existent and round and square. Thus something round and square exists although everything round and square is impossible. This ontological argument cannot be avoided by Kant's device of saying that existence is not a predicate. For [the Meinongians] admit that 'existing' applies when and only when being 'actual' applies, and that the latter is a *sosein*. Thus we cannot escape the consequence that the 'existent God' both exists and is God, and it is hard to see how it can be maintained . . . that this has no bearing on the question whether God exists.

Meinong could only reply that though God was existent, to be existent and to exist were not the same. Russell was surely right to be dissatisfied with such a reply.

Descartes, more consistent than Meinong, accepted the ontological argument; more cautious than Meinong, he is not vulnerable to Russell's argument about the round square. It is customary to dismiss Meinongian pure objects with a high-handed reference to their 'oddity', or by an appeal for 'a robust sense of reality'. Descartes would have regarded such a feeling for reality as a mere prejudice. More serious are the objections that such objects involve violations of the principle of non-contradiction. The round square, for instance, is both square (by definition) and not square (since whatever is round is not square).

Descartes could reply that this contradiction was the result, not of admitting pure objects, but of admitting impossible entities among them. Though Meinong did this, Descartes never did. He wrote: in the concept of every thing there is contained either possible or necessary existence (AT VIII, 2a, 60); what cannot exist therefore is no thing. 'Possible existence', he wrote, 'is a perfection in the idea of a triangle, just as necessary existence is a perfection in the idea of God; it is this which makes it superior to the ideas of those chimaeras whose existence is regarded as nil (*nulla*) (AT VIII, 383). He would not have been trapped by the argument that if a round circle is impossible, then there must *be* something (viz. the round circle) to be impossible. 'All self-contradiction (*implicantia*) or impossibility', he wrote, 'arises in our conception, which mistakenly joins together ideas which clash with each other. It cannot be situated in anything outside the mind, because if something is outside the mind, then *eo ipso* it is not self-contradictory, but possible' (AT VII, 152).

Descartes has an answer, too, to another argument suggested by Russell, namely that if existence is a predicate, than we can conceive an existent golden mountain, and this must in its turn exist. He appeals to the distinction between true and immutable essences on the one hand, and fictitious essences on the other. If F is part of the true and immutable essence of G it is impossible for us to conceive of a G which is not F. If, on the other hand, we can conceive of a G which is not F, then even though we can make up the notion of a G which is F, this will be a fictional essence and not an immutable essence. 'For example, when I think of a winged horse, or of a lion actually existing, or of a triangle inscribed in a square, I easily understand that I can on the contrary think of a horse without wings, of a lion as not existing and of a triangle apart from a square, and so forth, and that hence these things have no true and immutable essence.' An existent golden mountain, then, does not have a true and immutable essence, and therefore no conclusion can be drawn about its existence. God, unlike the existent golden mountain, is no fiction, because we can prove *a priori* that what has the properties of God has also existence though we cannot prove *a priori* that what has the properties of a golden mountain has also existence. None the less, if Descartes is to avoid the conclusion that the existent golden mountain exists, it seems that he must deny that there is any such thing as the existent golden mountain: he must exclude it from the realm of pure objects. I do not know of any place where he explicitly does so; but it is compatible with all the texts known to me. In conclusion, we may say that Descartes's argument is most intelligible if we regard him as admitting, with Meinong, that there is a status of pure objecthood, beyond being and not-being, but, unlike Meinong, denying this status to impossible and fictional entities, and restricting it to those entities which have true and immutable essences, i.e. those about which non-trivial truths can be proved *a priori*.

The most serious – indeed the insurmountable – objection to Meinongian pure objects is that it is impossible to provide any criterion of identity for them. If something is to be a subject of which we can make predications, it is essential that it shall be possible to tell in what circumstances two predications are made of *that same subject*. Otherwise we shall never be able to apply, for example, the principle that contradictory predications may not be made of the same subject. We have various complicated criteria by which we decide whether two statements are being made about the same actual man; by what criteria can we decide whether two statements are being made about the same *possible* man? The difficulties are entertainingly brought out in a famous passage in Quine's *On What there Is*.[8]

> Take, for instance, the possible fat man in that doorway; and again, the possible bald man in that doorway. Are they the same possible man, or two possible men? How do we decide? How many possible men are there in that doorway? Are there more possible thin ones than fat ones? How many of them are alike? Or would their being alike make them one? Are no *two* possible things alike? Is this the same as saying that it is impossible for two things to be alike? Or, finally, is the concept of identity simply inapplicable to unactualized possibles? But what sense can be found in talking of entities which cannot meaningfully be said to be identical with themselves and distinct from one another?

These objections are, I think, ultimately insurmountable and make untenable the notion of Meinongian pure objects: we may with

[8] *From a Logical Point of View*, Havard U.P., 1961, p. 4.

gratitude accept the alternative method of dealing with the non-existent offered, with the aid of quantifiers, by Frege and Russell. But it is perhaps worth remarking that when the pure object in question is God, then the difficulties about identification appear less palpable. For, in the nature of the case, only one omnipotent and all-perfect being is possible; so that we do not feel constrained to put to Descartes the question, '*Which* God are you proving the existence of?'

I shall not pursue these difficulties further in this paper, but I wish to conclude by drawing attention to a major difficulty internal to Descartes's own system. If the ontological argument is not to be a great *petitio principii*, it is essential that it should be possible to prove properties of the problematically existent. It must be possible, at least in some cases, to be sure that X is F without being sure that X exists. But if that is so, then what becomes of the *cogito ergo sum*? It is an essential step in the *cogito* that every attribute must belong to a substance. '*Pour penser il faut être*,' he says several times, is a necessary presupposition if the *cogito* is to work. And this is a particular example of a general principle, stated in the fifth definition of the *more geometrico* proof, and stated thus in *Principles of Philosophy* 1, II. 'It is very manifest by the natural light which is in our souls, that no qualities or properties pertain to nothing; and that where some are perceived there must necessarily be some thing or substance on which they depend.' But what right has Descartes to assume that the substance in question exists? If I can be sure that a triangle has its angles equal to three right angles without being sure that any triangle exists, why can I not be sure that *ego cogito* without being sure that *ego existo*? On the other hand, if I can argue, 'I think, therefore, I am,' why can I not argue, 'The triangle has three angles equal to two right angles, therefore the triangle exists?'

Perhaps I was incautious in saying that '*pour penser il faut être*' is a particular example of the principle of natural light. For what that principle shows us is that attributes cannot be attributes of *nothing*. But 'not to be nothing' and 'to exist' are not synonyms: does not Descartes speak of the ideas of 'things which even if they perhaps exist nowhere outside myself, cannot be said to be nothing'? (AT VII, 63) But if I was incautious, so is Descartes. In the exposition of the *cogito* in the *Meditations* itself, he trades on the two being equivalent: that deceiver 'nunquam efficiet *ut nihil sim* quamdiu me aliquid esse cogitabo'; and straightway he concludes to the truth of '*ego existo*' (AT VII, 25).

Descartes says that his system rests on two principles: his own existence and God's existence. If my account is right he cannot have both these principles in quite the way he wants them. If what does not exist can have properties, then he can perhaps prove God's existence, but he cannot prove his own. If what does not exist cannot have properties, he can perhaps prove his own existence, but he cannot prove God's existence by the ontological argument. The *cogito* and the ontological argument cannot both be valid.

11

Descartes's Ontological Argument Revisited[1]

In response to Professor Penelhum I should perhaps insist that I do not think Descartes's argument is valid. It fails, I contend, principally because Meinongian objects are indefensible. I agree with Penelhum that if we give Descartes enough rope he will hang himself; I was arguing merely that he should be given more rope than he is usually given.

Unlike Penelhum, I think that non-trivial *a priori* truths about God can be proved whether or not God exists. One such is mentioned by Malcolm: God cannot begin to exist. Anyone who finds insoluble the problem of evil must think that there are such truths: e.g. that no benevolent and omnipotent God could make a world such as the one we live in. It seems to me that these truths are not mere truths about language any more than Pythagoras' theorem is.

I agree with Penelhum that 'the geometer is not someone who invents but someone who discovers' is a less misleading way of saying part of what is meant by 'the triangle with its nature is *given*'. Existence theorems in mathematics prove, I think, what Descartes would call *givenness* rather than what he would call *existence*. In private conversation with Professor Körner after the meeting I came to see that the identity of essence and existence which, for

[1] The previous paper was delivered at a symposium at which it was discussed by Terence Penelhum, Norman Malcolm, Ernest Sosa and Bernard Williams. This paper is a reply to the criticisms made on discussions.

Descartes, was peculiar to God is in fact a feature of all mathematical entities as nowadays naturally conceived. This was not so for Descartes because of the concrete way in which he understood mathematical existence: for a triangle to exist is for there to be a triangular body; for a number n to exist is for there to be n concrete objects.

I do not follow Penelhum's argument that even if existence is a predicate it cannot be an essential one. I agree that existence could not be the *only* essential property of an object; existence, considered as a property, is as it were too thin to build up a nature. But if we accept that there are Meinongian objects, which can have, among their properties, that of existence, I do not see why there cannot be a Meinongian object to whom existence is essential. For Descartes the essence of an object is constituted by properties which it cannot cease to have: and any being which could cease to exist would not be God. I agree with Penelhum – and so, I have tried to show, would Descartes – that 'the notions of uncausedness and logically necessary being are quite independent'; but this tells not against Descartes's argument but against Malcolm's.

Professor Malcolm misunderstands my paper in seven ways.

(1) He says, 'Kenny concludes that a triangle might be given even if no one ever thought of a triangle'. I did not conclude this: I claimed that Descartes assumed it.

(2) He says, 'My first (small) comment is the Kenny has not made me understand what it is for something to be *given* without being *thought of*.' The main point of half my paper was that one must take this distinction seriously if one was to make sense of Descartes's argument. The main point of the other half of the paper was to say that the ultimate incomprehensibility of the distinction makes Descartes's argument fail. Much of Malcolm's first section is taken up with showing that what I said was (allegedly) true of given objects is false of objects of thought. I agree.

(3) Malcolm says that Descartes distinguishes between ideas as objects of thought and ideas as acts of thought. This is correct but irrelevant; for the idea of a chimaera is an object of thought no less than the idea of a triangle; but the triangle is given while the chimaera is not.

(4) Malcolm suspects 'that Kenny has made the error of

assuming that if one is thinking of a triangle, one must be thinking of a triangle *that exists*'. On the contrary, I take it as an obvious truth that one can think of what does not exist. One can also prove theorems about what does not exist. Meinong's assumption of pure objects was a faulty theory to explain the former truth; Descartes' assumption of 'given' objects was a misguided move to accunt for the latter truth.

(5) I do not see that Malcolm anywhere takes account of the remark I quoted from Descartes that my thought imposes no necessity on things. What, on Descartes's view, imposes necessity on my thought of a triangle when no triangle exists? To this question, I reply: the given triangle. Malcolm makes no reply.

(6) Malcolm says, 'If Descartes meant the subject of the sentence "God exists" to be something that is "beyond being", then he could not use the sentence to assert that God exists.' I do not think he can have noticed the passage I quoted from Meinong, that to say an object is beyond being and not being 'is not to say that an object can neither be nor not be'.

(7) Malcolm says he sees no merit in my 'claim that it is impossible to provide criteria of identity for objects of thought'. I made no such claim; I was talking about given objects, not objects of thought; and the passage I quoted from Quine concerned unactualized possibles. Malcolm's own criterion of identity for objects of thought seems much too strict: Malcolm and I are both thinking of the same thing if we are both thinking, say, of Bismarck; and this may be so without either of us 'stipulating' any properties for Bismarck.

The connection which Malcolm points out between the ontological argument and the doctrine of simple natures is, I think, very interesting and important. But I would like to see it made clear what is the relation between the simple *natures* of the *Rules* and the simple *notions* of the letters to Elizabeth. Are these entities identical? If so, are they mental or extra-mental? If not, are the former extramental and the latter their mental counterparts? One would needed to know the answer to these questions in order to assess the relevance of the doctrine to the interpretation of the Ontological argument.

It seems to me that one argument defended by Malcolm could be used to prove the necessary existence of all sorts of entities, e.g. of a hundred-year-old baby. It is inconceivable that a hundred-year-old baby should begin to exist; for if it began to exist, it would not be a hundred years old. Whatever can be conceived to exist but does not exist, can be conceived as beginning to exist, according to Anselm. Consequently, a hundred-year-old baby cannot be conceived to exist and yet not exist. If, therefore, a hundred-year-old baby can be conceived to exist, he exists of necessity. But there is nothing inconceivable in the notion of a hundred-year-old baby (why shouldn't a race take a very, very, long time to reach maturity?) Hence, a hundred-year-old baby exists necessarily. In this argument, one may substitute for 'hundred-year-old baby' any description such as 'Lucretian atom' or 'Aristotelean planet' and thus prove the necessary existence of anything which is by definition sempiternal.

Both Professor Sosa's points seem to be well taken. He is correct in pointing out that Descartes seems to have been unable to make up his mind whether a triangle inscribed in a square has a true and immutable essence. Perhaps this hesitation may be taken to indicate a dim perception of the problems of Meinongian status.

Sosa is also right that my formulation of the difference between true essences and fictitious essences is faulty. It might be amended to read as follows: 'Let E be an essence which can be defined by the predicates F and G, so that something possesses the essence E if it is both F and G. If F is part of the true and immutable essence E it is impossible for us to conceive of a G which is not F. If, on the other hand, we can conceive of a G which is not F, then even though we can make up the notion of G which is F, this will be a fictional essence and not an immutable essence.'

This will, I think, accurately reflect Descartes's view in the reply of Caterus. None the less, it will not save Descartes from Sosa's criticism, for a reason which was pointed out to me by my wife. On this criterion, a square will not have a true and immutable essence, as is clear if we let E be the essence of a square, and for F put 'equilateral' and for G 'rectangle'. This difficulty cannot be answered by distinguishing, as Sosa suggests, between simple and complex properties, unless we take the implausible view that *being triangular* is simple and *being rectangular* is complex.

12

The Cartesian Circle and the
Eternal Truths

In common with many other writers on Descartes, I owe a great debt to Professor Allen Gewirth's articles on Cartesian epistemology. In the first part of this paper I shall set out the extent to which I agree and disagree with him on the Cartesian circle: where I disagree, I shall be doing so on grounds, which I first came to appreciate through the study of his work. In the second part of my paper I shall develop a point only briefly mentioned by Gewirth, and shall connect the problem of the Cartesian circle with the doctrine of the creation of the eternal truths.

I

The problem from which Gewirth started in 'The Cartesian circle' was this.[1] Descartes seems to say both that present clear and distinct perceptions admit of no doubt, and that they are uncertain until guaranted by the veracity of God. This presents a dilemma, which forces itself on us when we consider the perceptions employed in the demonstration of God's existence. If these require the divine guarantee, then Descartes's argument is circular; if they do not, then he contradicts himself when he says that all perceptions required guarantee.

Gewirth's solution was as follows: He distinguished between

[1] A. Gewirth, 'The Cartesian Circle', *Philosophical Review* L (Oct, 1941).

psychological doubt (which is contrasted with the certainty of clear and distinct perception) and metaphysical doubt (which concerns the truth of what is clearly and distinctly perceived). Intuitions, he said, are not open to psychological doubt, but only to metaphysical doubt. Descartes's argument is not circular, because God's existence is proved by the psychological certainty of clear and distinct perceptions, whereas it is the metaphysical certainty of such perceptions that God's veracity guarantees.

I agree with Gewirth that the type of doubt that Descartes says is possible concerning clear and distinct perceptions is a different type of doubt from that which he says is impossible, so that there is neither contradiction nor circularity in his argument. Moreover, I agree with Gewirth, against defenders of the 'operational' or 'conceptual' interpretation of the doubt, that what is called in question by the doubting Descartes is not the genuineness of alleged clear and distinct perceptions, nor the conceptual warrants of the necessary connections of mathematics, but the truth of genuine, full-blooded, clear and distinct perceptions. Finally, I agree with Gewirth that Descartes's conception of truth was fundamentally a correspondence theory of truth and not, as some recent writers have implied, a coherence theory.

I think, however, that Gewirth's account of the contrast between psychological and metaphysical certainty is misleading. Consider the following crucial passage from the Third Meditation:

> When I considered something very simple and easy concerning arithmetical or geometric things, as that two and three make five, and the like, did I not intuit at least these sufficiently perspicuously, so that I might affirm them to be true?
>
> Indeed, I afterwards judged that these must be doubted for no other reason than because it came into my mind that perhaps some God could have endowed me with such a nature that I would be deceived even concerning those matters which seemed most manifest. But whenever this preconceived opinion concerning God's supreme power occurs to me, I cannot refrain from confessing that if he wishes, it is easy for him to bring it about that I err even in those matters which I think I intuit most evidently with my mind's eyes.

Yet whenever I turn my attention to those very things which I think I perceive very clearly, I am so completely persuaded by them that I spontaneously break out into these words: let whoever can deceive me, yet he will never bring it about that I am nothing so long as I think that I am something; or that it will sometimes be true that I have never been, when it is now true that I am; or perhaps that two and three make more or less than five and the like, in which matters I find manifest contradiction.

And certainly since I have no occasion for thinking that God is a deceiver, and since I do not even sufficiently know whether there is a God, the reason for doubting which depends only on that opinion is very tenuous, and, so to speak, Metaphysical. But in order that it too may be removed, as soon as the occasion offers, I must examine whether there is a God, and if there is, whether he can be a deceiver; for if this be not known, it seems that I can never be completely certain about anything else (AT VII, 35–6; HR I, 158–9).[2]

I agree with Gewirth that in the first and third of these paragraphs Descartes is expressing his psychological certainty of such propositions as that $2 + 3 = 5$, and that in the second and fourth paragraphs he is expressing his metaphysical doubt. But it is misleading to contrast metaphysical certainty with psychological certainty by saying that metaphysical certainty concerns *truth*. For psychological certainty also concerns truth: to be certain of something is to be certain that it is *true*. If Descartes's method is to be viable, clarity and distinctness must indeed be internal properties of ideas, as Gewirth says: but anyone whose ideas are clear and distinct cannot help but affirm the truth of what his ideas represent. As Descartes says in a passage quoted by Gewirth, 'I am of such a nature that so long as I very clearly and distinctly perceive something I cannot refrain from believing it to be true' (AT VII, 89; HR I, 183). Consequently, to express psychological certainty is to exclude doubt about the *truth* of the propositions

[2] In the present passage I have followed the translation given by Gewirth, except that I have replaced 'plainly' twice by 'completely' as a translation of '*plane*,' and have translated the *ipsas* in the first line of the third paragraph.

regarded as certain; concern for truth does not begin with what Gewirth calls 'the metaphysical moment'. Of course, the fact that I express psychological certainty that p does not guarantee that p is true; but neither does the fact that I express metaphysical certainty that p. Notoriously, some of the things Descartes was metaphysically certain about have turned out to be false.

How then is one to distinguish between metaphysical and psychological certainty? The answer is simple. Psychological doubt and metaphysical doubt are not, strictly, doubt about the same propositions. The propositions Descartes is psychologically certain about at the beginning of the Third Meditation are the particular propositions he clearly and distinctly perceives, viz. that $2 + 3 = 5$, that so long as I think I am something, I am not nothing. What Descartes is metaphysically doubtful about is the general proposition, that whatever he intuits most evidently is true. This general doubt may cast doubt on the particular propositions; but the doubt it casts is only a second-order, implicit doubt.

Look back at the passage from the Third Meditation, and you will see that the particular propositions of which Descartes is certain are not mentioned in the doubting paragraphs. This is no accident: if Descartes had mentioned them, he could not have doubted them. In the Second Replies he says:

> There are some propositions which are so perspicuous, and at the same time so simple that we can never think of them without believing them to be true: as that I, while I think, exist, and that what is once done cannot be undone. About such things we manifestly have a special certainty. For we cannot doubt of them without thinking of them, and we cannot think of them without believing them to be true (AT VII, 145–6; HR II, 42).

The examples given are the same as those in the Third Meditation. It could hardly be more clearly stated that such propositions can only be doubted at the price of not being mentioned while being doubted.

This passage in the Third Meditation, and a parallel one from the First, are summarized by Gewirth as follows: 'A valid metaphysical reason for doubting not only empirical propositions but even "very simple and easy" mathematical propositions like "2 + 3 = 5" and "a square has four sides" is the possibility that there is a God who deceives one'. But in neither passage does Descartes say that one can doubt that 2 + 3 = 5. In the First Meditation he says, 'How do I know that God has not brought it about that I am mistaken every time I add two and three together, or count the sides of a square, or do something simpler, if anything simpler can be imagined (AT VII, 21; HR I, 147). The sum of 2 and 3 is mentioned, but not used; the operation of addition is referred to, but not performed. Nowhere, however full of metaphysical doubt, does Descartes say, 'perhaps 2 and 3 do not make 5' or 'perhaps a square has five sides'. On his own theory, he could not say such things and mean them. And surely, on this point, his theory is perfectly correct.

Descartes can entertain the thought

(1) For some p, I clearly and distinctly perceive that p, but not p.

but he cannot entertain any thought that would be an existential instantiation of (1). He can also entertain the thought

(2) For some p, I clearly and distinctly perceived that p, but not p.

and he can entertain certain existential instantiations of (2). He says, for instance, in the Fifth Meditation,

> When I consider the nature of the triangle, it appears very clearly to me . . . that its three angles equal two right angles, and I cannot help believing this to be true as long as I attend to the proof; but as soon as I turn my mental gaze elsewhere, even though I may remember that I perceived it clearly, I can easily doubt whether it is true, if I am still in ignorance lof God (AT VII, 70; HR I, 184).

But this does not apply to simple and immediately obvious truths like those mentioned in the Third Meditation and Second Replies, which cannot be thought of at all without being believed. Even the most all-embracing doubt can touch these propositions only through referentially opaque wrappers. The doubting Descartes can do no more than say 'perhaps what I perceived five minutes ago is false' or 'perhaps I go wrong in what seems to me most evident'.

Consider the proposition, 'I cannot doubt what I clearly and distinctly perceive.' On Descartes's view, this is true if it means

(3) For all p, if I clearly and distinctly perceive that p, then I cannot doubt that p.

It is false if it means

(4) I cannot doubt that (for all p, if I clearly and distinctly perceive that p, then p).

The first and third of the paragraphs quoted from the Third Meditation illustrate (3); the second and fourth paragraphs give reasons for rejecting (4).

Is there an inconsistency in accepting (1) while rejecting every possible instantiation of it? Perhaps there is; but given the human condition it is a harmless and necessary inconsistency.[3] Every one of us, I imagine, would wish to subscribe to

(5) For some p, I believe that p, but not p.

Yet to accept any instantiation of this would involve one in a version of Moore's paradox. The inconsistency to which the doubting Descartes is committed is no worse than that of anyone who believes that some of his beliefs are false.

It is by now clear why there is no circle in Descartes's argument. The clear and distinct perceptions used in the proof of God's existence are perceptions of particular propositions, such as that ideas cannot be more perfect than their archetypes (AT VII, 42; HR I, 163). The veracity of God is used to establish not any

---

[3] It is akin to the logicians' omega-inconsistency. This point is made, with a misleading illustration, in my paper 'Happiness', *Proceedings of the Aristotelian society*, ns LXVI (1965/6), pp. 93–102, 95.

particular clear and distinct perception, but the general proposition that whatever I clearly and distinctly perceive is true.

The general proposition is first enunciated at the beginning of the Third Meditation (AT VII, 35; HR I, 157) after Descartes is already in possession of a number of particular clear and distinct perceptions. It is discovered, in accordance with Descartes's analytic method,[4] by reflection on the particular cases. Just as Descartes first discovered the principle 'whatever thinks, exists' in grasping the particular case of the *cogito* (AT VII, 140; HR II, 38), so in passing from 'I clearly and distinctly perceive that I am a thinking thing' to 'I affirm that it is true that I am a thinking thing' Descartes formulates the general rule that everything clearly and distinctly perceived is true. 'For it is the nature of the human mind to form general propositions out of knowledge of particulars' (AT VII, 141; HR II, 38).

On my account, there is no need, in order to exculpate Descartes from circularity, to appeal to the complicated analysis that Gewirth offered us. This analysis does not strike me as plausible. According to it, Descartes is uninterested in the truth of the proposition 'God is no deceiver' and seeks to show that it is clearly and distinctly perceived only in order to show that 'God is a deceiver' is not clearly and distinctly perceived. But nowhere does Descartes suggest that 'God is a deceiver' might be clearly and distinctly perceived.[5] Moreover, if 'God is no deceiver' may be clearly and distinctly perceived without being true, then all the other clear and distinct perceptions may be false too, the deceiving God having given me, among other deceptive perceptions, the deceptive perception that he is no deceiver – like a hypnotist hypnotizing me to forget that I have been hypnotized. Moreover, in order to get from ' "God is no deceiver" is clear and distinct' to ' "God is a deceiver" is not clear and distinct' one needs to make use of the premise that it is impossible clearly and distinctly to perceive contradictories. But on Gewirth's assumptions are we entitled to

---

[4] See the excellent account in 'The Cartesian Circle', pp. 375 ff.
[5] Descartes does say (AT VII, 21; HR I, 147) that there are '*validae rationes*' for the hypothetical doubt. But '*validae*' does not mean 'valid' in any technical sense such as Gewirth suggests, but merely 'strong'. At AT VII, 474; HR II, 277, Descartes explains that a reason can be *valida* while being *dubia*.

use this premise in the absence of a guarantee that clear and distinct perception involves truth? If not, then Descartes seems to be committing as great a circle in the assumption of this premise as the one Gewirth absolves him from.

So far, I have followed Gewirth in taking Descartes to be expressing fundamentally the same doubt in the Third Meditation as in the First. This procedure would be challenged by Professor Frankfurt, who in his recent book *Demons, Dreamers and Madmen* (Bobbs-Merill, Indianapolis, 1970) argues that clear and distinct perception is not considered by Descartes before the Third Meditation. 'It is essential to understand', he writes, 'that when Descartes discusses mathematical propositions in the First Meditation, he regards them as *not* being perceived clearly and distinctly' (*op. cit.*, 63).

In support of this contention Frankfurt quotes Descartes's remark to Burman that in the First Meditation he was considering a man who was first beginning to philosophize and had never considered axioms in the abstract (AT V, 146). He also quotes from the Seventh Replies: 'I once said in Meditation One that there is nothing about which one may not be in doubt, where I was supposing that I was not attending to anything that I perceived clearly' (AT VII, 460; HR II, 266).

Neither of the passages quoted by Frankfurt proves his point. The axioms Descartes was discussing with Burman are philo-sophical axioms, not simple truths of arithmetic. The remark from the Seventh Replies does not apply to the whole of the First Meditation, but only to the passage expressly quoted. It would apply equally well to the second and fourth passages quoted above from the Third Meditation, where Frankfurt agrees that Descartes is considering clear and distinct perception.

In several places Descartes explicitly contradicts Frankfurt's exposition. In the Fifth Meditation Descartes says:

> The nature of my mind is such that I could not help holding (geometrical truths) to be true so long as I perceive them clearly; and I remember that even at the time when I was most strongly immersed in the objects of sense. I counted as most certain those truths which I clearly recognized concerning

shapes, numbers, and other arithmetical and geometric matters, concerning pure and abstract mathematics (AT VII, 65; HR I, 180).

At the end of the Sixth Replies, he has this to say:

> Before I had liberated myself from the prejudices of the senses, I rightly perceived that two and three make five . . . Children no sooner learn to count two and three than they are capable of judging that they make five (AT VII, 445; HR II, 257).

In this passage, Descartes distinguishes between metaphysical truths (which children never think of) and the mathematical truths that Frankfurt lumps together with them. We know from the Second Replies that some truths are so simple that they cannot be thought of without being doubted. Those of such truths as are metaphysical may never have been thought of by a normal adult; but truths of simple arithmatic are on a different footing. Since these are so simple that they cannot be thought of without being clearly and distinctly perceived, and so useful that no one can live a normal life without paying attention to them, it follows that they are perceived clearly and distinctly by all normal adults. This is why Descartes takes mathematical certainty as the paradigm of the clarity and certainty his method offers.

II

Gewirth raises the question whether Descartes's doubt of mathematics is 'existential' or 'essential'. On the 'existential' account, the truth of mathematical propositions requires the existence of material objects, and Descartes's doubt about mathematics is part and parcel of his doubt about the material world. I agree with Gewirth in rejecting this interpretation. In the Sixth Replies Descartes says that we must not think that 'the eternal truths depend upon the human understanding or on any other existing thing' (AT VII, 456; HR II, 251).

I agree, therefore, with Gewirth that truth in mathematics

consists, for Descartes, in accordance with essences; but in several respects I wish to question his presentation of the 'essential' version of the mathematical doubt. First, it is misleading to present Descartes's ontology as a 'notion of nonexistent essences'. Descartes's theory, as I have argued elsewhere,[6] is one of nonexistent objects that *have* essences. Secondly, it is untrue that Descartes 'seems to veer between Platonic and Aristotelian interpretations of mathematical essences'. Descartes's philosophy of mathematics, as I shall show, is thoroughly Platonic: indeed he is the founder of modern Platonism. To show this, it is necessary to consider his theory of the creation of eternal truths.

On 15th April 1630 Descartes, nearing the completion of this treatise on physics, wrote to Mersenne as follows:

> The mathematical truths which you call eternal have been laid down by God and depend on Him entirely no less than the rest of his creatures. Indeed, to say that these truths are independent of God is to talk of Him as if He were Jupiter or Saturn and to subject Him to the Styx and the Fates. Please do not hesitate to assert and proclaim everywhere that it is God who has laid down these laws in nature just as a king lays down laws in his kingdom. There is no single one that we cannot understand if our mind turns to consider it . . . It will be said that if God had established these truths He could change them as a king changes his laws. To this the answer is: 'Yes he can, if His will can change.' 'But I understand them to be eternal and unchangeable.' – 'I make the same judgment about God.' 'But His will is free.' – 'Yes, but His power is incomprehensible' (AT I, 135; K, 11).[7]

In this letter Descartes writes as if it was 'an almost universal way of imagining God' to treat mathematical truths as independent of him. This was not in fact correct. In scholastic thought mathematical essences were independent of God's will, but were entirely

---

[6] See my *Descartes: A Study of his Philosophy* (New York, Random House, 1968), pp. 146–56.

[7] The scholastics preferred speaking of 'the essences of things' to using the Augustinian expression 'the eternal truths'; so much so that a writer like Scotus, discussing a passage where Augustine speaks of 'the incorporeal and eternal concept of a square', substitutes 'the essence of stone'.

dependent on God's essence.[8] Aquinas, for instance, discussing the nature of God's knowledge of the essences of creatures, says that, since the essence of God contains all that makes for perfection in the essence of every other thing, and more beside, God can know all things in his own essence, with a knowledge of what is proper to each (*S. Theol.* Ia 14, 5–6).

Mersenne himself, however, seems to have been prepared to defend the view that the mathematical truths were altogether independent of God; and in his next letter Descartes returned to the attack.

> As for the eternal truths, I say once more that they are true or possible only because God knows them as true or possible. They are not known as true by God in any way which would imply that they are true independently of Him . . . In God willing and knowing are a single thing, in such a way that by the very fact of willing something He knows it, and it is only for this reason that such a thing is true (AT I, 147; K, 13).

Why does Descartes say that the mathematical truths are 'true or possible' (*verae aut possibiles*)? One way of interpreting this would be in accordance with the 'existential' interpretation rejected by Gewirth: the eternal truths are true if there are material objects to be models for them; otherwise they are merely possible. But since Descartes believed that in fact there are no material objects corresponding to the Geometer's figures, actual bodies being too irregular (AT VII, 381; HR II, 227), and yet continues to speak of mathematical truths, which are true of these nonexistent objects (AT VII, 116–118; HR II, 20–21), the most consistent way to take the expression is as meaning 'true of actual or possible objects'.

Descartes's third letter to Mersenne on the topic begins:

> You ask me by what kind of causality God established the eternal truths. I reply: by the same kind of causality as he created all things, that is to say, as their efficient and total

[8] K = Descartes, *Philosophical Letters*, ed. A. Kenny (Oxford, 1970).

cause. For it is certain that he is no less the author of
creatures' essence than he is of their existence; and this
essence is nothing other than the eternal truths . . . I know
that God is the author of everything and that these truths are
something and consequently that he is their author . . . You
ask also what necessitated God to create these truths; and I
reply that just as He was free not to create the world, so He
was no less free to make it untrue that all the lines drawn from
the centre of a circle to its circumference are equal (AT I, 151;
K. 14).

After this letter we hear no more of the eternal truths until the
Replies to the Fifth Objections. Gassendi had objected to the talk in
the Fifth Meditation of 'the immutable and eternal nature of a
triangle'. It seems hard, he said, to set up any immutable and
eternal nature in addition to God. Descartes replied:

It would seem rightly so if the question was about something
which exists or if I was setting up something immutable whose
immutability did not depend on God . . . I do not think that
the essences of things and the mathematical truths which can
be known of them are independent of God, but I think that
they are immutable and eternal because God so willed and so
disposed (AT VII, 380; HR II, 226).

The Sixth Objectors too took exception to Descartes's doctrine.
The hand of Mersenne can be seen in the objections, which repeat
the language and queries of his letters of 1630 (AT VII, 417; HR
II, 237). Descartes's reply covers familiar ground; but a letter
to Mesland of 1644 adds some new points, including the
following:

. . . it was free and indifferent for God to make it not be true
that the three angles of a triangle were equal to two right
angles, or in general that còntradictories could not be true
together . . . Even if God has willed that some truths should
be necessary, this does not mean that he willed them
necessarily; for it is one thing to will that they be necessary,

and quite another to will them necessarily or to be necessitated to will them (AT IV, 110; K, 151).

Why did Descartes put forward the doctrine of the creation of eternal truths? Some have argued that in this Descartes was not really an innovator, but was merely following out later scholastic tradition. According to Koyré, for instance, Scotus and Ockham regarded truth in a manner analogous to Descartes as being dependent on the will of God.[9] The texts cited by Koyré, however, concern moral truth rather than metaphysical and mathematical truth. Scotus and Ockham are commonly said to have believed that things are good because God wills them, rather than that God wills things because they are good. But there seems no evidence that this voluntarism extended that dominion of God's will to mathematical, metaphysical and logical truths as well as to moral ones. It may be that some later scholastics took this further step; but in the Jesuit Suarez, the most influential scholastic of the generation preceding Descartes, the traditional doctrine is clearly affirmed again. In his treatise on God's knowledge, Suarez teaches that God knows essences simply by knowing his own essence and the ways in which it can be imitated. There is no trace in Suarez's teaching of eternal objects of God's knowledge distinct from God's own essence[10]

There are indeed two principal ways in which Descartes's doctrine differs from that of any scholastic he is likely to have read. The first is its Platonic aspect: the mathematical essences are distinct from the essence of God. The second is its voluntarist aspect: the mathematical essences are under the control of God's will.

Voluntarism in mathematics is rejected explicitly by Aquinas in chapter 25 of the second book of the *Summa contra Gentiles*.

Since the principles of some sciences, such as logic, geometry, and arithmetic are drawn solely from the formal principles which constitute the essences of things, it follows that God

---

[9] A. Koyré, *Essai sur l'idée de Dieu et les preuves de son existence chez Descartes* (Paris, Leroux, 1922), pp. 93–117.

[10] F. Suarez, *Opusculum de Scientia quam Deus habet de futuris contingentibus* (Salamanca, 1599), I, 4–5.

cannot do anything which conflicts with these principles: thus,
he cannot make a genus not predicable of its species, or bring
it about that the radii of a circle are not equal, or that a
rectilinear triangle should not have its three angles equal to
two right angles[11]

Platonism about essences is discussed in detail by Scotus in his
commentary on the thirty-sixth distinction of Peter Lombard's
Sentences (*Opera*, XVII, 445 ff.). There are certain people, Scotus
says, who divide things into three classes: (a) fictional beings;
(b) real beings with existence, or existential being (*esse existentiae*);
(c) real beings without existence. Even without existence, a real
being differs from a fictional being, in that it *can* have existence, and
therefore it has a certain absolute reality before it exists. This
absolute reality is called '*esse essentiae*': it reminds a modern reader
of the status of Meinong's pure objects, beyond being and non-
being. This belongs to it because of its relationship to an exemplar
in the divine mind: just as God is the efficient cause of the
existential being of things, so he is the exemplar cause of their
essential being.

The view here discussed clearly has similarities with that of
Descartes.[12] Like Descartes's mathematical entities, the things with
essential being are distinct from God, since they stand in a causal
relationship to Him. However, the relation is viewed as one of
exemplar causality, whereas Descartes viewed it as one of efficient
causality. 'God can be called the efficient cause (of the eternal
truths)', he said in the Sixth Replies, 'in the same way as the king is
the effector of the law, even though the law is not a physically
existent thing' (AT VII, 436; HR II, 251).

This Platonism is sharply criticized by Scotus. On this view, he
says, creation would not be creation *ex nihilo*. Something that has
essential being is, according to the theory, not nothing, and
creation would merely be the giving of existential being to what

---

[11] The chapter is quoted at length in Gilson's *Index Scolastico-Cartesien*, s.v. *Possible*.

[12] The view is often attributed to Henry of Ghent. Since Descartes is most unlikely to have
known the works of Henry at first hand, we need not explore the correctness of this
attribution. See Frederick Copleston, *A History of Philosophy* (London, Burnes-Oates, 1950),
vol. II, p. 470 ff.

already has essential being. The only activity of God that would really count as creation *ex nihilo* would be the production of creatures in their essential being; but this, according to the theory, is eternal, and so creation would be *ab aeterno*. On Scotus' own view creatures are the objects of God's ideas not according to existential being or essential being, but only according to an *esse diminutum* which corresponds to what a modern writer might call 'intentional' existence.

If Descartes ever read Scotus, therefore, he could only have got the doctrine of the eternal truths from Scotus' adversaries and not from Scotus himself. Though he denied to Gassendi that he was setting up anything eternal independent of God, he could not have denied that he was setting up something eternal *distinct* from God: this is why he can be called the father of modern Platonism. For ever since Augustine had identified the Platonic ideas with archetypes in the divine mind, no orthodox scholastic had ever admitted the existence of anything eternal except God and God alone. But for Descartes the geometers' triangle is an eternal creature of God, with its own immutable nature and properties, a real thing lacking only the perfection of actual existence (AT VII, 64; HR I, 121; AT VII, 116–118; HR II, 19–21; AT VII, 383; HR II, 228).

Among those who have admitted that Descartes himself originated the doctrine of the creation of eternal truths, some have suggested that he did not really believe it, but merely pretended to do so in order to please devout Christians by giving a theological foundation to his new and shocking physics. This seems unlikely. Descartes's doctrine, so far from being calculated to make him stand well with the Inquisition, was so dubiously orthodox as to lead him to ask Mersenne to try it out on people without mentioning the name of its inventor (AT I, 135; K, 12). He had intended to publish it in his treatise *Le Monde*; but after the condemnation of Galileo had alerted him to the dangers of associating theological opinion with physical theory, he laid aside the treatise and made no mention of the eternal truths in the *Discourse* or *Meditations*. He certainly regarded his theory as sound religious doctrine (he calls the contrary view 'blasphemy' to Mersenne), but he knew that in the theological climate of the time it would be more of a hindrance than a help to the acceptance of his philosophy.[13]

A more convincing religious motivation for the theory was suggested by Étienne Gilson, who drew attention to the influence exercised on Descartes in the 1620s by Oratorian theologians.[14] It was Cardinal Bérulle who convinced Descartes of his vocation as a philosopher, and it was the Oratorian Gibieuf to whom Descartes first announced his interest in metaphysics.[15] Moreover, Gibieuf's book of 1630, *De Libertate Dei*, was acclaimed by Descartes as agreeing entirely with his own view of God's freedom. The neo-Platonic doctrine of the divine simplicity, which Descartes appeals to in support of his theory in letters to Mersenne and Mesland, was a favourite theme of the Oratorian theologians.

The Oratorian influence is undeniable, but it does not seem adequate to explain Descartes's adoption of the doctrine. Descartes did not know of the existence of Gibieuf's book until after he had written his first two letters to Mersenne, and in any case the theory is not to be found in the book. The doctrine of divine simplicity is appealed to only as a second line of defence. The initial reason he gave for accepting the doctrine was that it was the foundation of his physics (AT I, 135; K, 11).

In what way did Descartes need the doctrine as a foundation for his physics? The answer is not far to seek. The prime novelty in Descartes's physical system was the rejection of the Aristotelian apparatus of real qualities and substantial forms: the first chapters of *Le Monde*, on which he was working at the material time, are a sustained polemic against these chimerical entities (AT XI, 3–36, and especially 37). Rejection of substantial forms entailed rejection of essences, since for Aristotelians the two are closely connected, essence being identical with form in the case of immaterial beings, and consisting of form plus the appropriate kind of matter in the case of material beings. Descartes did not reject the terminology of essence as firmy as he rejected that of form and quality, but he

---

[13] Gilbert Ryle once suggested that the Cartesian consciousness is the Lutheran conscience laicized (*Concept of Mind*, New York, Barnes & Noble, 1959, p. 139). With equal warrant one might speculate that the creation of eternal truths is the secularization of the Calvinist doctrine of God's absolute sovereignty.

[14] *La Liberté chez Descartes et la Théologie* (Paris, Alcan, 1912), pp 157–210.

[15] J. R. Vrooman, *René Descartes: A Biography* (New York, Putnam, 1970), pp. 75–9.

reinterpreted it drastically. When, in his letter to Mersenne of 27 May 1630 cited above, he says that the essences of creatures are nothing but the eternal truths, he is throwing over the idea that an essence might be a principle of explanation, an element in the constitution of a substance which might have causal effects on the history of the substance (as, for example, the essence of an oak might be thought to provide an explanatory factor in the life-cycle of an oak).

Now in the Aristotelian system it was the forms and essences that provided the element of stability in the flux of phenomena which made it possible for there to be universally valid scientific knowledge. Having rejected essences and forms, Descartes needs a new foundation for the certain and immutable physics that he wishes to establish. If there are no substantial forms, what connects one moment of a thing's history to another?

The immutable will of God, replies Descartes, who has laid down the laws of nature, which are enshrined in the eternal truths (AT VII, 80; HR I, 192; AT XI, 37). These laws include not only the laws of logic and mathematics, but also the law of inertia and other laws of motion (AT III, 648; K, 136). Consequently they provide the foundations of mechanistic physics. The physics is immutable, because God's will is immutable.

But might not God have immutably willed that at a certain point in time the laws might change – just as Descartes wrote to Mesland that God contingently willed the laws to be necessary (AT IV, 110; K, 151)? If this possibility is to be ruled out, not only God's immutability but also God's veracity must be appealed to. God would be a deceiver if, while giving me such a nature that I perceive these laws as immutable, he had also decreed that the laws were to change. So the veracity of God is not only sufficient, but also necessary, to establish in Descartes's post-Aristotelian system the premanent validity of clearly and distinctly perceived truths.

It will now be clear why I reject Gewirth's claim that there is in Descartes's account of mathematics an Aristotelian strain. Gewirth cites passages in favour of the view that 'mathematical essences . . . are not independent of physical existents, but the mathematician deals with them as if they were independent' (p. ix above). The passages cited support the view that the objects of mathematics are not independent of physical *substances*; but they do not support the view that the objects of mathematics depend for their essences on physical *existents*. Gewirth appears to confuse the distinction between substance and mode with the distinction between possible and actual existence. (To see the difference, bear in mind that neither Pegasus not Pegasus's shape exists; but Pegasus is a non-existent substance, whereas Pegasus's shape is a nonexistent mode.) Descartes held that a geometrical figure was a mode of physical or corporeal substance; it could not exist, unless there existed a physical substance for it to exist in (AT VIII, 26–7; HR II, 241–2). But whether it existed or not, it had a kind of being that was sufficient to distinguish it from nothing, and it had its eternal and immutable essense.

The Aristotelian view which Gewirth attributes to Descartes, that there cannot be essences of things that do not exist, does indeed appear in Descartes's published works, but from the pen of Hobbes, in the Third Objections. 'If a triangle exists nowhere at all', Hobbes wrote, 'I do not understand how it can have any nature; for that which exists nowhere does not exist. Hence it has no existence or nature . . . The nature of triangle will not last for ever, for if every triangle whatsoever perished, it would cease to be.' Descartes rejected this suggestion with contempt (AT VII, 194; HR II, 77).

It is misleading to call Descartes's mathematical objects, as Gewirth does, 'abstractions'. No doubt all Gewirth means is that mathematical objects are incapable of existing apart from sub-stance; but the term suggests that the notion of these objects is acquired by a process of abstraction. This, of course, is something that Descartes consistently denied, on the grounds that there were (for example) no existing triangular substances for abstraction to acquire the notion of triangle from (AT VII, 381; HR II, 227).

13

The Cartesian Spiral

In my book *Descartes* (New York, Random House, 1960, pp. 172–99) and in a paper published in the *Journal of Philosophy* in 1970 I presented an account of the alleged circle of Descartes's *Meditations*. In the present paper I wish to defend that account against a number of criticisms subsequently published, and to take the consideration of the Cartesian circle to a more profound level.

My account of the matter went thus. Descartes seems to say both that present clear and distinct perceptions admit of no doubt, and that they are uncertain until they are guaranteed by the veracity of God. What of the propositions used in the proof of God's existence? If they require a divine guarantee, then the argument is circular; if not, this is inconsistent with the view that all perceptions require a guarantee. To solve this difficulty, and following Gewirth, I made a distinction between psychological certainty and metaphysical certainty; I read the passage in the beginning of the Third Meditation as expressing psychological certainty of propositions such as $2 + 3 = 5$ (clear and distinct perceptions) and read the metaphysical doubt as an expression of doubt whether psychological certainty guarantees truth.

Strictly speaking, psychological doubt and metaphysical doubt are not doubt about the same propositions. The propositions that Descartes is certain about at the beginning of the Third Meditation are the particular propositions he clearly and distinctly perceives, e.g. that $2 + 3 = 5$, that as long as I think I am something I am not nothing. What he is metaphysically doubtful about is the general proposition, that whatever he intuits most evidently is true. The existence of the general doubt casts a certain doubt on the particular propositions, but only a second order, implicit doubt: Descartes cannot attend to the propositions themselves and at the same time doubt them.

Is there an inconsistency in believing whatever he clearly and distinctly perceives, while doubting whether whatever he clearly and distinctly perceives is true? At most, I suggested, only a harmless omega inconsistency: the kind of inconsistency involved in saying 'I believe that some of my beliefs are false'. There is no circularity in the proof of God's existence, because the proof depends on particular intuition, and the conclusion of the proof is used to establish only the general proposition, that whatever I clearly and distinctly perceive is true.

Alan Gewirth[1] objected to the idea that because clear and distinct perceptions are psychologically certain they stand in no need of any divine guarantee as to their metaphysical certainty. The difference between psychological and metaphysical certainty is this:

> For p to be metaphysically certain means that there is no possibility of doubting rationally at any level, direct or indirect, whether p is true: that is, not only are the intellectual requirements fulfilled which were referred to in connection with psychological certainty, but in addition there is no possibility of any *ex post facto* doubt of p on the ground that there might be a radical disparity between the structure of the mind that asserts p and its purported objects. In these terms, then, the whole point of Descartes's metaphysical doubt is that, so long as there is a possibility that God is a deceiver, psychological certainty is not the same as, and provides no definitive warrant for, metaphysical certainty. Consequently Kenny is mistaken if he thinks that the psychologically certain propositions used to prove God's existence are, at the time they are so used, metaphysically certain and hence in need of no guarantee by God.

[1] 'Two Disputed Questions', *Journal of Philosophy LXVII* (1970), 66–70.

What, Gewirth asks, is the relation between the metaphysical doubt concerning the general proposition and the psychological certainty of the particular ones? If the particular clear and distinct perceptions are open even to second order doubt, they are not metaphysically certain and cannot be used to establish God's existence in a definitive way. It is true that one can be certain that some clear and distinct perceptions are true without being certain that all clear and distinct perceptions are true; but this does not help here.

> On this interpretation . . . the 'whatever' or 'all' in Kenny's general proposition would signify merely a collective or enumerative universal; that is, in the proposition 'it is doubtful that all clear and distinct perceptions are true' what would be meant is that the doubtfulness attaches not necessarily to each clear and distinct perception taken distributively, but rather to the sum total of clear and distinct perceptions, such that while some clear and distinct perceptions are indeed certain, we don't know whether all the others are, and hence in this sense whether all are. This collective interpretation is not however a correct rendition of Descartes's position.

Gewirth asks whether, according to Descartes, the psychological certainty that p is true entails the metaphysical certainty that p is true. Of course the answer is no, since in order to be metaphysically certain a proposition must be incapable of being rationally brought within the scope of an *ex post facto* doubt of the truth of all clear and distinct perceptions. Gewirth is wrong to suggest that I think that the psychologically certain propositions used to prove God's existence are at the time they are so used metaphysically certain: I think that the question 'Are they metaphysically certain at the time they are used?' is a confused one. If it means 'Can they be subjected to the *ex post facto* general doubt at the very moment of their perception?' then the answer is obviously no: perceiving them in particular and doubting them in general are two different and incompatible activities which cannot be carried on at the same moment. On the other hand it is also clear that the fact that they are now being perceived with psychological clarity does not exclude their being later doubted under some general description such as 'what I clearly and distinctly perceive'.

Gewirth's question whether 'what I clearly and distinctly perceive' is to be taken collectively or distributively seems to betray a misunderstanding of the nature of universal affirmative propositions. The appropriate question to ask is whether the expression should be taken to be referentially opaque or referentially transparent. If it is taken to be transparent, then I cannot doubt what I clearly and distinctly perceive. If it is taken opaquely, then I can doubt what I clearly and distinctly perceive. It is the *ex post facto* opaque doubt which is the metaphysical doubt that a proof of God's existence and truthfulness is supposed to lay to rest.

Feldman and Levison[2] see an inconsistency between my statement 'the truth of particular intuitions is never called in question' and my other statement 'no axioms are immune to second order doubt' . . . the second order doubt is precisely the question whether first order indubitability is compatible with falsehood'. They are right to say that Descartes can, in a roundabout way, call in question the truth of the simplest particular intuitions. My point would have been better put by saying that simple axioms cannot be doubted in any way which involves advertence to their content. They can be doubted, individually as well as generically, under a definite description: for instance, I may wonder whether the first axiom to appear on page one of the Meditations is false. This is a roundabout doubt, because it cannot be based on any reason connected with the content of the proposition doubted. It must be based on some general reason, for instance the possibility of creation by a deceitful god. It was this that led me to say, incorrectly, that simple axioms could only be doubted generically, not severally: Feldman and Levison are correct to take me to task for this.

In my reply to Feldman and Levison in the same journal, I said that though Descartes could raise the individual roundabout doubt he does raise only the generic one; but that too was incorrect: he

---

[2] 'Anthony Kenny and the Cartesian Circle', *Journal of the History of Philosophy* IX (1971), p. 491 ff.

says in the Seventh Replies that I may go wrong when I add two
and three together (VII, 476).

Feldman and Levison quote, from the Third Meditation:

> When I was considering some very simple and very easy point
> in arithmetic or geometry, e.g., that two and three together
> make five, did I perceive this clearly enough to assert its truth?
> My only reason for judging afterwards that it was possible to
> doubt these things was that it occurred to me that perhaps
> God could have given me such a nature that I was deceived
> even about what seemed most obvious.

This passage in fact confirms the idea that never in Descartes is
there a proposition that at a given moment is both intuited and
suspected to be false. Descartes says that he judged *afterwards* that it
was possible to doubt simple and easy points in mathematics; and
he doubted them under a generic description 'what seemed most
obvious'.

Descartes thought that doubt was impossible without a reason.
The only reason for doubting what seems most obvious is the
second order, general, reason of the possibility of creation by a
deceiver. Once Descartes has demolished this reason by proving
that existence of a truthful God, he disposes of the general doubt
and of any particular roundabout doubt based only on general
doubt. Descartes's speculation has as its aim to make it the case
that he should never again have reason to change his mind about
what he had once intuited. But this is not incompatible with its
having as its aim to establish or discover a certain truth. By
establishing the truth of the proposition 'I am the creature of a
truthful god' Descartes is at the same time trying to make it true
that he will no longer have any reason for doubting his intuitions.

It is undoubtedly correct that even proof of a veracious deity is
insufficient to establish immutable certainty: even if the proof can
be so mastered as to be surveyable in a single glance of intuition, it
needs supplementing with an infallible memory if it is to prevent
me doubting the truth of conclusions whose proofs I no longer
recall. Otherwise 'I clearly and distinctly perceived once that *p*; but
God is no deceiver; ergo *p*' goes lame. But this is a criticism of

Descartes, not of my interpretation of him. In both the second and the sixth replies Descartes says that no one can have immutable and certain knowledge unless he first acknowledges that he has been created by a truthful God. My claim was only that Descartes's argument was not circular; I have never claimed that it was adequate.

Harry Frankfurt has argued, in a number of papers, and in his book *Dreams, Demons and Madmen*, that Descartes can be acquitted of circularity only if we regard his procedure as aiming not to show that what is intuited is true, but simply that there can be no reasonable grounds for doubting it. The sceptic seeks to show that reason leads to falsehood by showing that it is inconsistent; Descartes can prove that it is coherent without at any point appealing to its truth, and thus he avoids circularity. I have argued elsewhere that Frankfurt's interpretation does not accord with Descartes's text.

Frankfurt finds my own solution unhelpful for the following reasons:

> If Descartes is to establish the certain truth of his conclusion, he must provide true premises whose truth is reliably guaranteed; and it must be possible for him to provide his guarantee for the premises without relying on the assumption that the conclusion is true . . . Whether the premises are true . . . depends upon whether what leads Descartes to believe the premises is a reliable guide to truth. But what leads Descartes to believe that premises of his argument is just that he perceives them clearly and distinctly. And whether the fact that he does so entails their truth is a question which depends precisely on whether the conclusion of the argument is true or false. (*Dreams, Demons & Madmen*, 66)

Frankfurt's criticism depends on a confusion between cause and reason, masked by his use of word 'depend'. It is as a matter of fact false that whether the premises are true depends upon whether what leads Descartes to believe the premises is a reliable guide to truth; this is not true whether 'depend' is taken either as causal or as logical dependence. But I will not dwell on this because I think

Frankfurt's argument could be expressed as well if the word 'certain' were substituted for 'true' and with this substitution his claim becomes more plausible. The equivocation takes place in the next two sentences. What *causes* Descartes to believe the premises is his clear and distinct perception of them; he is not led to believe them by a process of reasoning which includes, among its premises, 'I clearly and distinctly perceive these premises'. But this is what is suggested by Frankfurt's next sentence 'whether the fact that he does so *entails their truth* [my italics] is a question which depends precisely on whether the conclusion of the argument is true or false'. Frankfurt, like many other authors, thinks that Descartes is trying to produce reasons for trusting intuition. In fact, Descartes is doing exactly the opposite. He is trying to enable us to intuit that we can trust reasoning: more precisely, that we can trust the conclusions of reasoning when we have ceased to intuit the premises and the entailment of the conclusion by the premises.

Frankfurt is critical of my introduction of 'omega doubt', the kind of doubt illustrated by saying 'I believe some of my beliefs are false'. He says, 'Kenny cannot maintain that Descartes is entirely satisfied with the reliability of his particular intuitions and at the same time maintain that Descartes entertains omega doubts concerning them.' I do not maintain that at all. Descartes is not perfectly satisfied with the reliability of his particular intuitions because he is, before the proof of God, vulnerable to *post facto* metaphysical doubt about them. What I do maintain is that it is a consistent position to say: perhaps some of the things which, whenever I think of them, I am unable to doubt, are false or 'perhaps some of my most certain beliefs are false'. I think it is not only consistent but rational to consider this possibility; and personally I believe that some of the things about which I'm absolutely certain are false.

But if Descartes never doubted particular simple clear and distinct perceptions, such as $2 + 3 = 5$, how can he say, in a much quoted passage (VII Objections, AT VII, 477) that before going through the purification of Cartesian doubt hardly anyone has ever perceived anything clearly? The necessary qualification is added immediately: 'with that clarity, at least, which is necessary for metaphysical certainty'. The clarity which is needed for metaphysical certainty is clarity sufficient to rebut the metaphysical doubt which is the second order doubt about the trustworthiness of clear and distinct perceptions in general.

Here is relevant the passage in the Sixth Replies about the atheist mathematicians. An atheist, said the objectors, asserts that his knowledge that if equals be taken from equals the remainders are equal is absolutely certain; 'for he cannot frame those statements mentally without believing them to be absolutely certain' (AT VII, 414). Descartes in reply did not suggest that an atheist might doubt these propositions while thinking of them, or that his perception of them was not clear and distinct; he simply repeated that the atheist might wonder whether he has so imperfect a nature 'as to be deceived in matters which appear most evident to him' (VII, 428).

More clearly still, in the Second Objections, Descartes did not deny the possibility that an atheist might clearly and distinctly perceive that the three angles of a triangle are equal to two right angles; he simply said that the atheist's knowledge could not be called real science, since it could be called in question by the general doubt whether he was not deceived in those things which seemed most evident to him (AT VIII, 125, 141). In the case of a complicated geometrical proof the atheist can doubt the conclusion when he is no longer attending to the chain of argument (AT VII, 70); but in the case of something as simple as '$2 + 3 = 5$' even this possibility is ruled out.

I conclude then that even someone in the position of the inquirer of the first Meditation has clearly and distinctly perceived that $2 + 3 = 5$ and that he can only doubt this in a roundabout way by turning his attention elsewhere and concentrating on the possibility of an omnipotent deceiver who may deceive him even in the things which appear to him most evident.

There remains one passage which is difficult to fit into my account. Bourdin, the author of the Seventh Objections, tells the story of a man who, half asleep, heard a clock strike four and said, 'The clock is going mad: it has struck one o'clock four times.' Descartes replied that this story showed that a person who adds two and three together can be deceived by an evil spirit. It is hard to see how, on any account, the story shows what Descartes says:

the man is not making a mistake in addition, but is misjudging the intervals between the strokes; the error is not in the arithmetic but in its application. Perhaps the truth is that the nearest Descartes can get to giving an actual example of an error in a clear mathematical judgement is to give an example of an error in its application: this is sufficient, *ad hominem*, to Bourdin who does not distinguish pure and applied arithmetic. To be sure, to be able to doubt that *p* and to be able to err in thinking that *p* are two different things: so there is anyway no inconsistency between what Descartes here says and the account that I have given above.

It is beyond doubt that the faculty of clear and distinct perception is *used* in order to establish the principle that whatever is clearly and distinctly perceived is true. I think that this is probably what really worries people about the Cartesian circle, and this worry is not laid to rest by showing that there is no circular argument in Descartes (as I claim to do). It is not laid to rest, either, by claiming in the manner of Frankfurt that Descartes is not trying to show that whatever is clearly and distinctly perceived is true (in any ordinary sense of 'true') but merely that whatever is clearly and distinctly perceived is coherent. Let me see if I can do anything to meet the worry: for it is this worry that takes the problem of the Cartesian circle to another level and makes it a Cartesian spiral.

It has often been observed that when Descartes is calling into doubt whatever can be doubted he does not call into doubt his own knowledge of language. It has less often been observed – it was first observed in my hearing by Dr J. Cohen of Birkbeck College – that if Descartes had called it into doubt, he could have used an argument rather like the *cogito* to set the doubt at rest. Suppose that there is some deceiver, supremely powerful, supremely intelligent, who purposely always deceives me: perhaps he is only deceiving me into thinking that I understand language. Well, let him deceive me as much as he may, he will never bring it about that, at the time of thinking that I understand language, in fact, I do not understand language. I must conclude that this proposition 'I understand language', whenever I utter it and conceive it in my mind, is necessarily true. For if it is false, the thought that it is the case is one which I cannot have; perhaps, like a parrot, I can utter the sounds 'I understand language', but they cannot be the expression of a thought and so, *a fortiori*, cannot be the expression of a false thought.

This argument is one which is parallel to Descartes's vindication of reason as understood by Frankfurt. For its conclusion, you will notice, is not that 'I understand language' is true, but simply that the truth of 'I understand language' cannot be questioned by the most powerful methods of questioning that can be devised; for the obvious enough reason that the method of questioning – any method of questioning – must itself presuppose the truth of the conclusion it purports to question.

I do not myself think that the argument is a very close parallel to the validation of reason, since I think that the validation of reason is meant to establish the truth of a general proposition which can be brought into question without self-contradiction. I wish to use it merely to show one thing. I think it is an unquestionably valid argument, involving no circularity; yet it is clear that the ability to understand language is something that is *used*, and used without hesitation, throughout the construction of the argument.

To make an exact parallel to the way I believe Descartes's argument goes one would have to construct a different, less plausible, counterpart.

(1) I understand the sentence I am now uttering.

(2) Whoever understands a single sentence understands a whole language.

(3) Therefore, I understand a whole language.

Again, we have an unquestionably valid argument. The lack of plausibility resides in the second premise: in order to be convinced of this one needs to reflect on fairly abstruse considerations of the type advanced by Chomsky or Wittgenstein. However, the lack of intuitive plausibility does not harm the example; for it seems to me no more and no less likely that reflection on the arguments of Wittgenstein or Chomsky might lead one to intuit the truth of (2) than that reflection on the Third and Fourth mediations may lead one to believe in the existence of an undeceiving God.

Would Descartes himself have thought that there was a vicious circularity in using a faculty to vindicate its own reliability? He would certainly have disapproved of the suggestion that one could use the faculty of sight to vindicate its own reliability, using, say, the deliverances of close-up vision to correct and control those of distant vision. Even close-up vision, he says, needs checking in the light of a higher, more reliable faculty: it is that which tells us to believe touch and not sight when a stick half-immersed in water looks bent and feels straight.

It seems that if he is to be consistent without being circular, he must regard the faculty operative in simple clear and distinct perceptions as a faculty different from that operative in those perceptions which can be doubted. If these are two different faculties then there is not even the secondary kind of circularity – the spiral circularity – which consists not in arguing to a conclusion from a question-begging premise, but in using, to validate the reliability of a faculty, the faculty itself in question.

What answer would Descartes give to the question: is the faculty of clear and distinct perception of simple truths the same as that used on comparatively remote conclusions from axioms? No doubt he would have contemptuously dismissed the question as a piece of Aristotelian logic-chopping. But the question is important for the internal coherence of his own system. In this as in other respects Descartes suffered from his contempt for Aristotle. But we cannot afford to sneer at him, any more than he could afford to sneer at Aristotle. The question of the individuation of faculties, abilities and powers is one of the great uncharted areas of modern philosophy. Until a few years ago it was hardly regarded as a serious philosophical issue at all. And if it is now taken seriously by some philosophers, that is not thanks to any philosopher, but to the linguist Chomsky, who has made respectable the notion of faculty psychology. It is both ironic and fitting that this problem, which is crucial to the Cartesian system and was neglected by Descartes himself to his cost, should be resurrected by the most distinguished of those who, in the present age, are willing to call themselves Cartesians.

Index